DIVING OFFSHORE CALIFORNIA

DIVING OFFSHORE CALIFORNIA

By Darren And Stacey Douglass

AQUA QUEST PUBLICATIONS, INC. ▪ NEW YORK

PUBLISHER'S NOTE

The Aqua Quest *Diving* series offers extensive information on dive sites as well as topside activities.

At the time of publication, the information contained in this book was determined to be as accurate and up-to-date as possible. The reader should bear in mind, however, that dive site terrain and landmarks change due to weather or construction. In addition, new dive shops, restaurants, hotels and stores can open and existing ones close. Telephone numbers are subject to change as are government regulations.

The publisher welcomes the reader's comments and assistance to help ensure the accuracy of future editions of this book.

Good diving and enjoy your stay!

Library of Congress Cataloging-in-Publication Data

Douglass, Darren.
    Diving offshore California / by Darren and Stacey
    Douglass.
        p.   cm.   — (Aqua Quest diving series)
    Includes index.
    ISBN 0-9623389-5-8 : $18.95
    1. Scuba diving—California—Channel
Islands—Guidebooks. 2. Channel Islands (Calif.)—Description
and travel. I. Douglass, Stacey, 1960-
II. Title. III. Series.
GV840.S78D67   1992
797.2'3—dc20   91-71780
                                    CIP

Printed in Hong Kong
10 9 8 7 6 5 4 3 2 1

Cover: *Offshore California offers a wealth of opportunities for the adventuresome diver.*

Title page: *An inquisitive sea lion approaches the camera in a bed of giant kelp.*

All photographs are by Darren Douglass unless otherwise noted.

Maps by Justin Valdes

ACKNOWLEDGEMENTS

Without the insight and support of these friends, this book could not be possible: Captain Phil Bardini, Tony Bliss, Carl Boyer, John Brumm, Bonnie Cardone, Captain Glenn Fritzler, Larry Hagebusch of Tabata, John Hardy, Captain Roy Hauser, John Hayes of Oceanic, Captain Tom Healy, Captain John Hess, Captain Roger Hess, Kathy Hill, Roy Hinrichs, Shuichi Ishikawa, Captain Bill Johnson, Captain Arnold Lancaster, Ken Loyst, Steve Maderas, Lee Petersen, Jens Rubschlager, Dale and Kim Sheckler, Steve Whitaker, the Captains and crews of Truth Aquatics, the staff of the Channel Islands National Monument and a special thanks to the entire southern California dive boat fleet.

In memory of our friends

Jack McKenney
Joe and Janet Ream

CONTENTS

Foreword

Like many other argonauts who venture
seaward in search of adventure and new
experiences, we might be so bold as to claim
that we truly know these offshore islands,
pinnacles and banks. In over 12 years of
diving, we have visited them during all kinds
of conditions, and experienced the best and
worst these waters can muster. Some days the
dive boat skims along a flat ocean and
dolphins jump along the bow. On other days,
the boat tops the crests of churning ten-foot
swells as the exposed twin propellers give off a
high pitched whine. We have felt the cold
blast of gale-blown water, the sun's warmth
reflecting on our wet suits, and heard the
rasping blast from the blow hole of migrating
gray whales.

Fortunately, most of the time the sea and sky
are fair and experiences predictably tame, but
all the while memorable. From the placid kelp
beds of San Clemente in summer to the ocean-
fed pinnacles at San Miguel in fall, diving
offshore California has special rewards
unparalleled in the diving world.

Yet, as we anchor for the night in Tyler Bight,
listening to 700-pound elephant seals barking
and yapping on the distant beach, we realize
how few of the many nuances of this offshore
life we really understand.

This saga is true for all the world's oceans,
for the sea is ever changing and its inhabitants
always fascinating. No matter how many visits
a diver makes to the sea, new discoveries are
constantly revealed. It is a humbling and awe-
inspiring experience even for seasoned divers.

It is in this light that we share what we have
learned about the islands and banks in our
great front yard of the Pacific. It is not an
exhaustive overview by any means; for every
site listed there are scores remaining. This
guide is a practical sampling to enable all of
those who love the ocean to explore and probe
further into this wonderful world.

Darren and Stacey Douglass
February 1992

"Your path led through the sea,
your way through the mighty waters,
though your footprints were not seen."
—Psalm 77:19

CHAPTER I   A COASTAL OVERVIEW

THE PAST

California has a rich history of early explorers, missionaries, pirates, fur hunters, whalers, and gold seekers. From its early days as a Spanish Colony and then as a part of Mexico to its incorporation into the United States, Californians have always displayed an air of independence. Perhaps this was due to the area's isolation from other populated regions.

The intertidal zone with its abundant fish, lobster and abalone was a productive source of food for the early Indian inhabitants of the California coast long before European explorers arrived.

Juan Rodríguez Cabrillo was the first European to peer through his spyglass at the golden state. Cabrillo, a Portuguese employed in the service of Spain, marched with Hernan Cortes during the conquest of Mexico. Rumors of Indian cities made of gold were prevalent among the conquistadors of the day. Driven by an insatiable lust for more wealth, land and sea expeditions were dispatched to the far reaches of the North American continent.

Viceroy Antonio de Mendoza sent Cabrillo to sail northward out of the port of Navidad, Mexico in 1542. Cabrillo's commission was to reconnoiter the Pacific side of the Spanish Main and sail further westward in search of the fabled Strait of Anian that was rumored to lead to the Orient and all its riches.

Cabrillo never returned to Mexico. After pressing his badly fitted ships into head winds along the southern California coast, he discovered several offshore islands. Cabrillo's caravels wintered at Cuyler Harbor on San Miguel Island where they were met by the large population of natives living on the island. After spending some time on San Miguel, Cabrillo suffered a severe fall, breaking his arm near the shoulder. Despite his accident, Cabrillo gave orders to sail northward, continuing the search for the Strait of Anian,

beating windward towards Cape Mendocino. After returning to San Miguel Island, Cabrillo died on January 3, 1543. His dying orders were for the expedition to proceed northward one more time in search of the Orient.

His pilot, Bartolome Ferrer pushed the ships and scurvy-stricken men onward toward the northwest before returning to Mexico. While Cabrillo did not find riches similar to those of the Aztec Empire in Mexico, he opened a sea route to a new world.

As Spain's slow and inefficient colonization process began on the West Coast, visiting American and British vessels were eyed with suspicion. Yankee ships from Boston, as well as French, English, German and Russian ships engaged in sealing, whaling and otter-hunting expeditions. To offset this threat, presidios (military garrisons), pueblos (towns) and missions were established along the Camino Real. Mixed caste soldiers and Mexican-born Indians were encouraged to populate California and offered tax-free inducements to become settlers.

Spain's attempts at colonization were only partially successful and most of the coastal pueblos and presidios were often ill equipped. While the Missions flourished through the efficiency of Franciscan friars and the toil of their Indian laborers, garrisons became so badly outfitted at San Francisco and Santa Barbara that many a rusting canon was unable to fire a salute to passing ships.

Pink gorgonians are a common sight in the waters surrounding California's offshore islands.

But before long, an era of clandestine trade developed between the Californians and the Yankee traders from Boston. New England ships brought shoes, cloth and furniture in exchange for tallow and hides. Richard Henry Dana's immortal classic, Two Years Before the Mast chronicles these adventures. This trade, and the whaling and fur hunting, was not without risks. Out at the Channel Islands, the unwary trapper could find his vessel incarcerated by a Spanish gunboat and quickly stripped of its earnings. Despite the threat of capture when bypassing the customs houses of San Diego and Monterey, the trade continued, with many smugglers using the coastal islands as hideaways as well as a source of water and wood. This commerce continued even when California became a part of Mexico.

The Present

Today, with the onset of urban sprawl, California strikes a marked contrast to its earlier years. Yet, as one moves closer to land's edge, it is possible to mentally brush the buildings and traffic out of the picture—even in Metropolitan Los Angeles. Clear winter days still offer the romance of walking down a crisp, deserted beach with the snowcapped peaks of the Angeles National Forest towering high above the San Gabriel Valley. The closer one stands to the water, the farther the concrete maze of Hollywood and Santa Monica Boulevard slide into the distance.

Offshore California is the same steel blue sea that drew explorers of centuries past, and still beckons modern-day adventurers.

California's offshore resources continue to provide for many residents. Commercial fishermen bring home full loads of abalone, sea urchin, crab and lobster from the islands. Drilling rigs pump precious oil from deep beneath the seabed between Point Conception and Huntington Beach. Supertankers in Long Beach and Los Angeles harbors unload Alaskan crude oil. Car carriers from the Orient deliver hundreds of Hyundais, Hondas and Nissans.

Yet twenty to one hundred miles offshore, the underwater world of the coastal islands and outer banks remain largely as they did when Cabrillo sailed past them for the first time in 1542.

Certainly, some environmental damage has occurred in areas of overfishing and heavy diver traffic. But the whale and otter are no longer hunted, other measures to protect marine life are in effect, and divers are showing more environmental awareness than in the past. Hopefully, with wisdom and foresight, future visitors will be able to see offshore California in much of the same way that Cabrillo did—as a rich, unspoiled and diverse ecosystem offering abundant rewards for those who venture leagues away from land.

Useful Information

Island tours. There are numerous sources of information on the offshore islands listed in Appendix 3. The National Park Service and some private concessions offer land tours of the various islands which can be an unusual diversion for divers who have spent years seeing an island from the waterline down. Some islands, such as Santa Barbara, Anacapa and San Miguel feature primitive campsites. The island of Santa Cruz has bunkhouse accommodations in one of the Vail and Vicker's ranch buildings. Other places listed in Appendix 3 have displays of natural and man-made history of the islands.

Shore landings. Visitors should be aware that certain islands are off limits to the public. Military islands, such as San Nicolas and San Clemente expressly prohibit landing, with violators facing immediate arrest. Landings are allowed at certain parts of Catalina Island. The islands under control of the National Park Service allow landing in one degree or another. Environmentally sensitive islands such as San Miguel will only permit visitors under the escort of a ranger.

Landing on almost the entire West Anacapa Island is prohibited to protect nesting brown pelicans. These pelicans were almost decimated in the 1970's due to the effects of DDT. Some regulations are in force year round while others are seasonal. Be sure to get current information before landing.

Aircraft regulations. Aircraft are required to maintain altitudes of 1000 feet when flying over the islands to protect sea birds and avoid disturbing wildlife.

Unpredictable weather. Whether diving, boating, or hiking, bring layers of warm clothes, a hat, sunglasses and sunscreen. Weather is unpredictable, so be prepared for anything. If camping on an island a warm sleeping bag is necessary. For overnight dive boat trips, blankets are provided in the bunkroom, but during cold periods these may not be enough. Many divers bring their own sleeping bags on boat trips as well.

Southern region. Before sailing for San Nicolas or San Clemente Islands check the weekly *Notice to Mariners* issued every Friday by the U.S. Coast Guard. Certain areas of these two islands are periodically put off limits when the U.S. Navy conducts live firing exercises.

Northern region. If hiking along island trails, stay clear of cliffs as erosion can make these areas unstable and dangerous. Remember, the famous Spanish explorer Juan Rodríguez Cabrillo died in 1543 from injuries sustained in a fall on San Miguel Island.

And, while on East Anacapa Island, keep well away from the lighthouse. Its high intensity foghorn can permanently damage one's hearing.

The rocky coastlines of California's offshore islands provide divers with an opportunity to explore a wealth of fascinating underwater terrain. This is the backside of Santa Catalina Island.

CHAPTER II DIVING

Each island off the California coast has its own unique character and personality. Some are remote and defiantly inhospitable. They are swept by prevailing winds and pounded by strong ocean swells. Low-lying sand dunes, weathered ridges, scrub brush and a terrain of sedimentary rocks all add to the sense of isolation. Other islands are closer to the coast, less foreboding and more frequently visited by divers.

WEATHER

Weather patterns along the California coast are always unpredictable. From Point Conception to the Mexican border, it is possible on a sunny afternoon for divers at San Clemente Island to relax in warm sunshine with not so much as a ripple of wind when only forty miles away at Cortes Bank, foreboding clouds blow like fast moving phantoms across the surface of the water and large swells roll through the shallows. Here, the sea quickly turns into a vicious foaming arena few watercraft would dare to enter.

Monitoring marine radio is helpful and usually provides an accurate account of conditions. However, there have been days when dive boats anchor in fair, sunny weather without a trace of wind, while the crew in the wheelhouse listens to a report of small craft warnings and heavy seas in effect for their immediate area.

When a high pressure system has been in the region for several days, one can almost be assured of small swells and fair weather at sea.

When Santa Ana winds (strong, warm winds blowing offshore from the desert) prevail, calm leeward anchorages can become dangerous for improperly anchored craft as wind-generated waves can throw them onto the rocks. Under these conditions, the traditional windward sides of the islands suddenly become the protected side.

To visit the outer pinnacles, banks and oil rigs, better than average conditions are required to avoid a bone-jarring boat ride and heavy surge at the dive site.

For divers, the California coast has few seasonal fluctuations as conditions are generally mild. They can, however, change rapidly. A dive boat venturing seaward in light rain and heavy fog can return with a suntanned group of passengers that experienced a wonderful day of diving. By the same token, there has been more than one vessel churning to the islands on a bright sunny morning when ferocious winds and high seas suddenly appear.

Many California divers consider fall and winter to offer the best diving conditions because upwellings contribute to excellent visibility during those times. Although water and air temperatures begin to drop at this time of year, overall weather patterns remain relatively stable and predictable. Unless large southerly swells are present in the fall, or westerly to northerly swells in the winter, offshore diving can be spectacular. Usually, only one or two major winter storms blow through the area each year allowing for excellent diving most of the remaining time.

Conditions during spring months are often considered to be marginal, but surprises do occur. In the spring, winter run-offs from streams, cliffs and rivers can obscure coastal water visibility. Another condition specific to, but not limited to, this time of year is plankton bloom. While the bloom occurs during a similar time frame it will affect different areas. For example, some parts of Catalina may be hard hit with 10- to 15-foot visibility during a plankton bloom, whereas San Clemente Island

Diving through a forest of kelp is an experience no visitor to the offshore islands should miss.

Seasonal Differences*		
Season	Visibility (feet)	Surface Water Temperature (degrees F)
December-March	40-80	54-60
April-May	20-60	52-56
June-August	60-90	65-75
September-November	80-150	62-68

*Visibility and temperature can vary widely depending on depth and local conditions.

may have clear, 100-foot plus visibility. Most rainstorms also arrive during spring.

Summer is a season when most divers go diving, not a season when the best diving occurs. But warm temperatures will always get divers thinking about hitting the water again thereby resulting in many charter boats running full from Memorial Day to Labor Day. Visibility is good in the summer, but not always the best. Water temperatures are comfortable though, and save for a few periods when southerly swells are present, summer offers enjoyable diving.

ACCESS

To access the marvels of the offshore California world, a seagoing vessel of some sort is required. Catalina Island provides land-based diving opportunities at the Avalon Underwater Park, but divers must still take the ferry over from the mainland.

SNORKELING (S)

Many offshore dive sites are also excellent for snorkeling. They are identified by an (S) after the name of the site and in the Table of Contents. If you are planning on making a snorkeling trip on a commercial boat, be sure to check beforehand what sites will be visited.

Entry and exit procedures may differ slightly on different boats.

BOAT DIVING

The best way to visit offshore California is to sail aboard one of the many commercial dive vessels that carry passengers seaward on a daily basis. To find a reliable dive boat, refer to Appendix 4 or contact one of the dive centers in Appendix 5. The captains and crews of these boats are experienced hands who will get divers to the sites and go out of their way to make sure the experience is pleasant and memorable. Most dive boats average from 60 to 80 feet in length and are designed to accommodate all types of weather. The boats feature warm bunkrooms, galleys for a variety of hot meals, showers, and ample deck space to store dive and camera gear. Most run multi-day as well as single-day trips.

There are specific techniques involved in diving off a boat in California waters. Here are some tips to help make dive boat trips to the offshore sites a success.

Don't Forget Anything

It can be annoying watching others dive while sitting on the boat because of a forgotten wet suit, mask, glove or other piece of equipment. Pack your gear in an unhurried manner well before heading to the boat. Be sure you have your C-card, as well as money to pay the galley bill and air fills. If you are planning on taking game you must have a current California ocean fishing license.

Bring Plenty of Spares

Divers should always bring spare items, especially on multi-day trips. Fin and mask straps, spare gloves, masks, snorkels, o-rings, and even an extra regulator come in handy at times. If using camera equipment or dive lights, spare bulbs, batteries and lots of film are helpful.

Load Time

Arrive at the landing at least one hour before departure. This insures you will be able to board on time, stow gear and park your car without having to rush. Then sign in on the manifest (print your name clearly) and/or check in with the divemaster.

Use Gearbags

Always work out of your gearbag. On a small (or even large) boat it is easy to get sloppy and misplace gear. It is also a good idea to make sure your gear is well marked for easy identification.

Air Fills

If you are on a boat and air fills are not included on the trip, be sure to mark your tank with a piece of masking tape including your name and manifest number. Unmarked tanks will not be filled.

Store all of your dry clothes below decks. As a rule, dive boats do not allow wet suit-clad divers in the bunk room. The crew will be happy to fetch anything you may need from the bunk room, but to be sure these items are readily accessible, leave them in a small backpack in the galley. And remember, all dive gear stays topside. No scuba equipment of any kind is allowed below deck.

Dive Profile

Every diver is responsible for his own dive profile, whether using computers or tables. If unsure of your calculations, ask the divemaster for assistance.

Photographers Beware

When making a nightime crossing to the outer islands, photographers should tape their assembled cameras down on galley tables with masking tape. Occasionally, even during calm conditions, a rogue swell is encountered which could send unsecured cameras and lenses flying through the air with expensive results!

Seasickness

The offshore islands are surrounded by open ocean and subjected to the full force of the wind and swells. Calm conditions can deteriorate rapidly so be sure to take a preventive seasickness medication.

Gear Storage

All scuba hardware stays on deck. Keep tanks and weight belts out of the galley at all times. If you have any questions as to exactly where to stow your gear, check with the divemaster or crew; they will be glad to assist you. Never leave an unsecured tank on deck. It could easily fall over and injure someone.

Night diving can open up a whole new world to the diver as marine life hidden during the day ventures out to feed.

Descents and Ascents

The easiest manner in which to descend and ascend is to follow the anchor line. It provides a visual reference and allows divers to slow down while equalizing.

In heavy swell conditions when the anchor line is jerking up and down, it can literally beat you black and blue. Stay neutrally buoyant and let the line slide through your hand if you are doing a safety stop. A diver that stubbornly hangs on during "bucking bronco" conditions could dislocate a shoulder or be pulled rapidly to the surface and be at risk of embolizing. The tightening and slackening of the anchor line can also catch onto gauges, cameras and tank valves. Divers must always evaluate the sea state and use common sense before holding the anchor line. Under really rough conditions when the anchor line is bouncing, it may be best to use it as a visual reference only.

Dive Partners

Go through a complete check of each others' gear before hitting the water. Discuss the standard procedure for buddy separation: look for no more than one minute then surface. This allows separated teams to regroup quickly rather than having to scour the bottom in search of one another.

Entry

When approaching the entrance gate, all your gear should be in place except fins. You put your fins on, jump into the water, and quickly swim out of the way to give the next diver a turn. This reduces crowding at the gate.

Recall Systems

Many dive boats have underwater recall systems. These are used if there is an emergency on board, or if the anchor drags. When you hear the recall (usually a siren-type sound), surface cautiously, look toward the boat and follow the crew's instructions.

Currents

Currents are often present when diving offshore. Not only can they change velocity, but they can also change direction during a dive. While diving in kelp beds, the kelp plant itself becomes a current indicator. Like a weathervane, if the kelp is bending back over your head and trailing behind you, you are diving up current as you should during the beginning of the dive. Any time that you are swimming in the same direction the kelp is lying, unless heading back towards the boat, you should reevaluate your heading; you are probably navigating down current. If not a planned drift dive, you will have a lot of work ahead of you in getting back to the boat.

A current line is deployed off the stern of the boat, with a buoy attached at the end. This is helpful should a diver surface down-current. If conditions preclude visual contact with the buoy, look towards the boat for directions to the line. Once on the line, you can pull yourself back to the boat.

Air Consumption

Watch your air consumption. There is no excuse for running out of air. If diving in thick kelp, leave extra air for navigating back to the boat underwater thus avoiding surface entanglements.

Spearguns

Spearguns should be kept unloaded when entering and exiting the water and anytime you are within 75 feet of the boat. Without proper precautions spearguns can be extremely dangerous.

Watch Out for the Boat

Avoid swimming just beneath the surface of the water when returning to the boat. Another dive boat's propellers can inflict serious injury should you cross its path.

During the swim back to the boat, keep your mask on and watch the movement of the boat and water. Occasionally, wind, swell and waves can make boarding the exit ramp difficult. Keep your regulator handy as sometimes the wind can blow the boat right over you, requiring a quick descent to avoid getting smacked.

When conditions are rough, time the swell action and climb on the boat's ladder when at its lowest point. Be prepared to hang on when the swell rises. Climb onto the ramp and hand cameras and unloaded spearguns to a crewmember. Remove your fins before climbing the ladder from the ramp into the dive boat.

Secure Your Gear

Once aboard, stow all of your equipment inside your gear bag. This keeps the deck clear for other divers and prevents equipment loss. If making another dive, tag your tank for airfill.

Unloading

Be sure you unload all your equipment from the boat at the end of the trip. Gear left on board is often difficult to recover.

PRESERVING RESOURCES

Many sites in this book are excellent producers of halibut, rockfish, scallops, abalone and lobster. While we prefer to hunt with cameras, our own table has been graced many times with a gourmet dinner from the sea.

However, we strongly advocate the sensible and lawful taking of game. Offshore California has tremendous diving and game taking resources. A caring, intelligent hunter or photographer can successfully meet his objectives without spoiling the environment. Listed below are some useful guidelines for maintaining our resources.

Game

- Always have a current California Department of Fish and Game license when taking game.
- Know and observe current California Fish and Game regulations and remember that different rules may be in effect for specific areas. If in doubt about a regulation, ask the captain or crew.
- Know what species you are taking. If you are unsure of the species do not take it.
- Use an approved caliper to measure lobster and abalone underwater. Don't bring "shorts" back to the boat. If the specimen is too small to take, put it back where you found it. Tuck lobsters back inside their holes so they won't fall prey to sea lions and sheepshead. Press abalones onto the rock and wait a few seconds until it resecures itself.
- Take only what you and your immediate family and friends will consume. Don't stock up the freezer.
- Avoid waste! If storing limited supplies of game in the freezer, wrap thoroughly with several layers of butcher's paper, aluminum foil or plastic bags to eliminate "freezer burn" that will spoil your catch. When packaged properly, frozen seafood can be stored for several months.
- Clean fish promptly after taking it. This preserves the freshness of the meat and prevents fillets from acquiring a fishy taste.
- Use a sharp knife when filleting fish to avoid leaving food on the bone and wasting it. A one square inch patch of

skin must be left on the fillet so the game warden can identify the species.

- Only take abalone with an abalone iron. Do not use a knife as abalone are hemophilic. Once cut they will quickly bleed to death and die.
- Many of southern California's offshore dive sites are sought after for their large plate-sized rock scallops. In the past many divers pried the entire scallop off the reef itself, killing numerous cohabiting organisms and damaging the reef. To avoid this damage the following practice is recommended by the operators of Truth Aquatics dive boats:

  - Bring a small game bag, pry bar (either an abalone iron or knife) and a small, sharp fillet knife.
  - Pry the scallop open by using your pry bar as a wedge between the two half shells.
  - Take the small fillet knife and sever the muscular foot as close to the flat side of the shell as possible.
  - The scallop will pop open allowing the collector to remove edible portions and dispose of the waste. This leaves the

scallop shell in place and prevents damage to the reef and the surrounding animals.

Low-Impact Diving

- Marine organisms are intrinsically interdependent on one another. Damage to any organism will affect other species as well. Many are slow growing. The purple hydrocoral, for example, grows at a rate of about an inch a year. A single swipe of a fin or knock from a dangling console can cause years of damage to the environment.
- Avoid being overweighted.
- Be sure to maintain neutral buoyancy to prevent accidentally banging into the reef.

Artifacts

Removing artifacts or damaging shipwrecks within the Marine Sanctuary (Santa Barbara Channel Islands) or within three miles of the coast and six miles from any island in the Sanctuary is strictly prohibited. Officials are vigilant and all divers caught violating these regulations face stiff penalties. Those interested in such activities should apply for a permit from the State Lands Commission, or look elsewhere.

Spearfishing is a popular activity and can be deliciously rewarding.

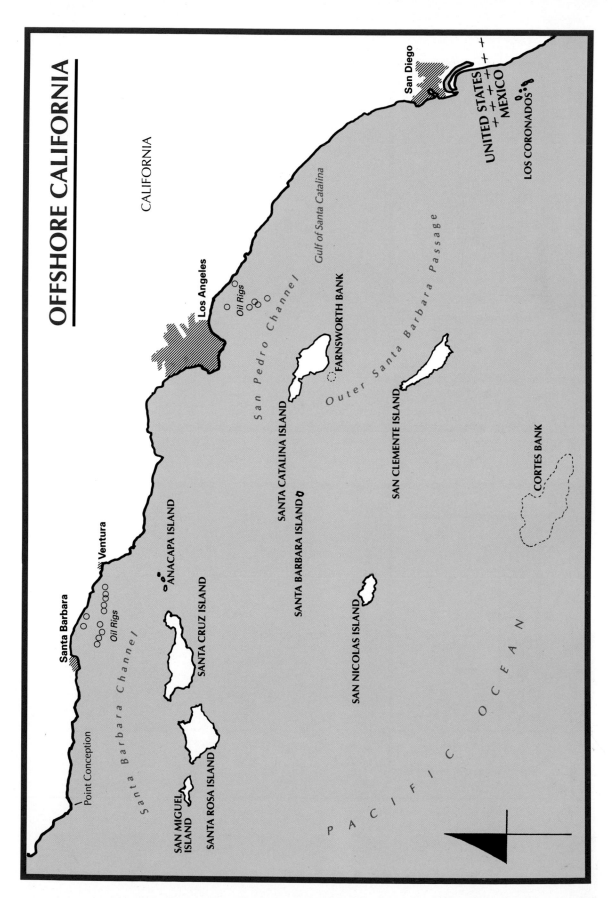

OFFSHORE CALIFORNIA

CALIFORNIA

Los Angeles

Oil Rigs

San Pedro Channel

Gulf of Santa Catalina

San Diego

UNITED STATES

MEXICO

LOS CORONADOS

FARNSWORTH BANK

SANTA CATALINA ISLAND

Outer Santa Barbara Passage

SAN CLEMENTE ISLAND

CORTES BANK

Ventura

Santa Barbara

Oil Rigs

Point Conception

Santa Barbara Channel

ANACAPA ISLAND

SANTA CRUZ ISLAND

SANTA BARBARA ISLAND

SAN NICOLAS ISLAND

PACIFIC OCEAN

SAN MIGUEL ISLAND

SANTA ROSA ISLAND

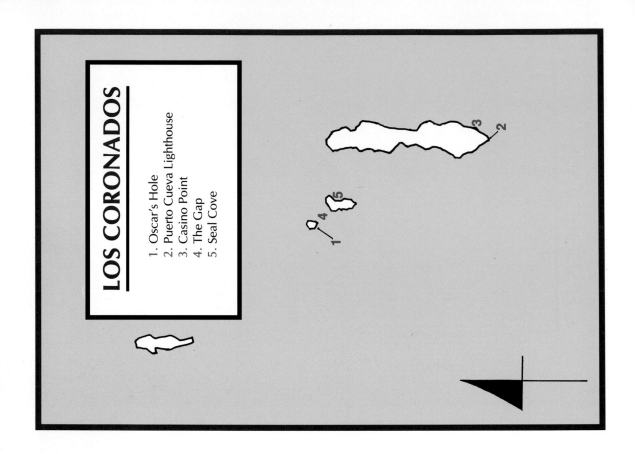

LOS CORONADOS

1. Oscar's Hole
2. Puerto Cueva Lighthouse
3. Casino Point
4. The Gap
5. Seal Cove

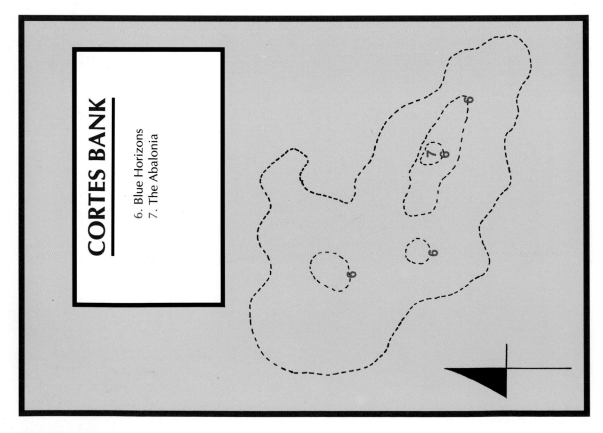

CORTES BANK

6. Blue Horizons
7. The Abalonia

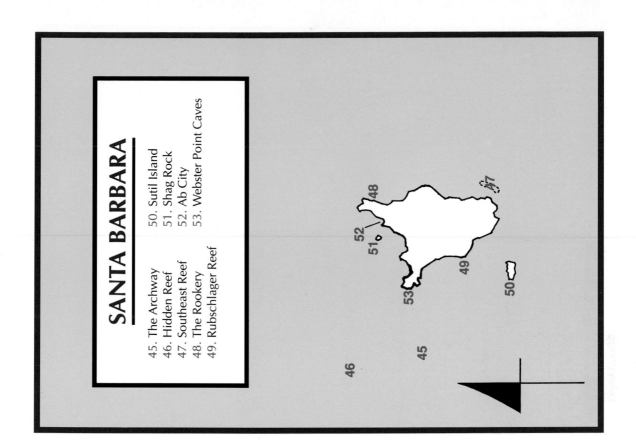

SANTA BARBARA

45. The Archway
46. Hidden Reef
47. Southeast Reef
48. The Rookery
49. Rubschlager Reef

50. Sutil Island
51. Shag Rock
52. Ab City
53. Webster Point Caves

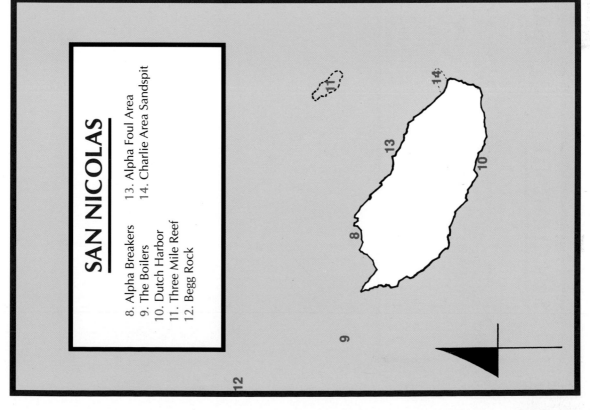

SAN NICOLAS

8. Alpha Breakers
9. The Boilers
10. Dutch Harbor
11. Three Mile Reef
12. Begg Rock

13. Alpha Foul Area
14. Charlie Area Sandspit

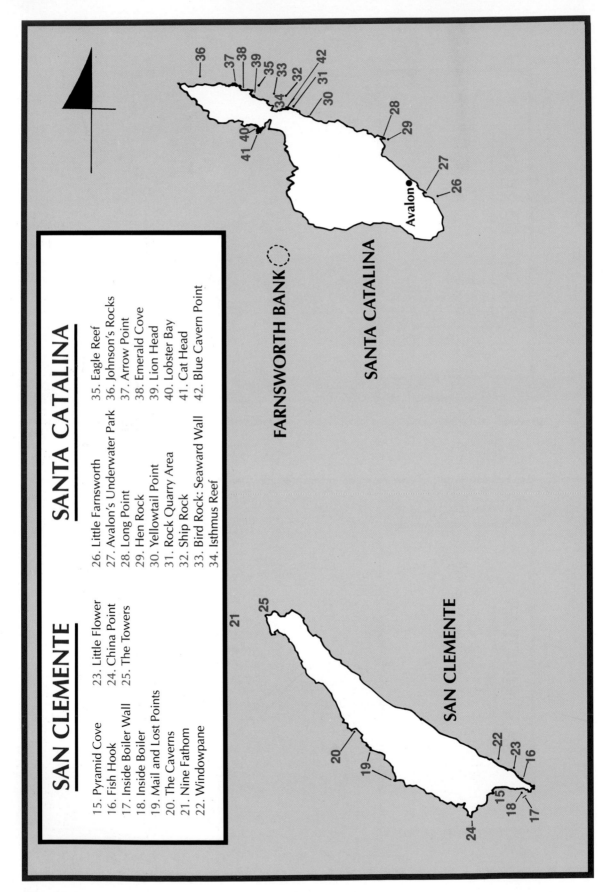

SAN CLEMENTE

SANTA CATALINA

FARNSWORTH BANK

SANTA CATALINA

Avalon

SAN CLEMENTE

SAN MIGUEL

83. Wilson's Rock
84. Richardson's Rock
85. Simonton Cove
86. Cuyler Harbor
87. Wyckoff Ledge
88. Point Bennett Foul Area
89. Skyscraper
90. Whistle Buoy
91. Boomerang Bank

SANTA ROSA

73. East End Pinnacles
74. East Point Shallows
75. Johnson's Lee
76. The Chickasaw
77. Talcott Shoals
78. Carrington Point
79. Rodes Reef
80. Brockway Point
81. Becher's Bay
82. Skunk Point

SANTA CRUZ

63. Forney's Cove
64. Morse Point
65. Gull Island
66. Profile Point
67. Painted Cave
68. Laguna Harbor
69. Willows Anchorage
70. Yellow Banks
71. Scorpion's Anchorage
72. Southeast Scorpion

ANACAPA

55. Arch Rock
56. Cathedral Cove
57. East Fish Camp
58. Coral Reef
59. Cat Rock
60. West Anacapa Cliffs
61. Frenchy's Cove
62. Footprint Reef

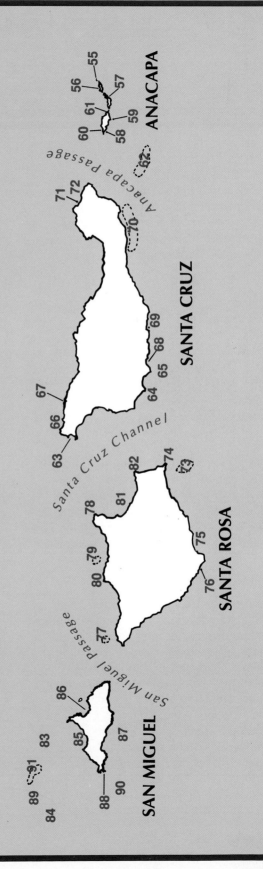

CHAPTER III   LOS CORONADOS

Refer to map on page 22.

Thirteen miles south of San Diego is a small cluster of islands called the Coronados that attracts divers and fishermen from both the United States and Mexico. The Coronados belong to Mexico and are only a short boat ride off the California coast.

HISTORY

The log of Spanish explorer Sebastian Vizcaino, who stopped at the Coronado Islands in November of 1603, contains the first known European record of the islands. This desolate string of three islands provided anchorages for occasional whaling and sealing ships in the 1800's.

It was during the prohibition years, from 1920-1933, that the Coronados gained renown. At the height of this period, a hotel and casino flourished on the islands.They provided a variety of vices including gambling, rum and prostitution to numerous American visitors. Today, the former resort structures are inhabited by families of Mexican fishermen.

GEOGRAPHY

The Coronados are a group of three small islands and a wash rock. This isolated outpost in Mexican waters has long been a favorite of American divers and fishermen. Each island has unique characteristics and features.

The closest island to the United States is Coronado Del Norte (North Coronado). From the distance, the island, ringed by cliffs and surrounded by deep water, appears foreboding. It is difficult to find good anchorages which limits diving to the experienced only. Coronado Del Norte is well known by discerning and experienced divers for its caves, steep ledges, walls and excellent visibility.

Farther southeast lies the largest island in the chain, Coronado Del Sur (South Coronado).

During hot, dry months, the treeless island appears barren, desolate and forlorn. Its low-lying shores jut sharply forming a series of V-like escarpments along the higher cliffs, adding a slightly inhospitable touch. Two small lighthouses located along the high ridges aid navigators through this potentially perilous combination of rocks and water. During the rainy season the island's hillsides turn green with grass intermingled with patches of wildflowers.

The island's waterline, however, is where nature's abundance begins. The shores are teeming with intertidal marine life, including a variety of marine birds, mammals and schools of fishes.

Perhaps the most intriguing area within the island group is Coronado Del Medio, known as Middle Grounds. Squadrons of pelicans and other seabirds wheel above the waves and dive-bomb the abundant schools of fishes. The rocky promontories at Middle Grounds are relatively small, offering few sheltered lees for boats.

DIVING

On a typical early summer morning, the three islands are usually shrouded behind a hazy veil. Seemingly primordial, the steep cliffs loom out of the mist like a shadowy apparition as surge pounds the washrocks with brine.

While the Coronados may be small in size, they certainly offer a diversity of diving opportunities. Each weekend during the season, dive vessels of all sizes—mostly from San Diego—converge on the area. Many fishing boats also cruise in an out of the

This mosaic of brittle stars, sea urchins, mussels and anemones is typical of the rich marine life blanketing most reefs.

Coronados so the surface traffic can be heavy at times. Divers should use caution when surfacing if the sound of whirring boat propellers is present.

When swells are present, surge can be quite strong at depth, but this presents few problems to the diver who is relaxed and goes with the flow. When seas are calm, however, dive boats can pull right up to the long rocky ledges and finger reefs. There is excellent diving to be found along the drop-offs.

There are some important items that American divers need to bear in mind. First, the taking of abalone and scallops is strictly prohibited. Additionally, all divers venturing seaward on charter boats will be required to purchase a Mexican fishing license whether they take game or not. There are excellent opportunities for both exploration and photography in the Coronados.

While the Coronados are a distance from the nearest neighboring island in the southern Channel islands chain, they should not be overlooked. One does not have to go any farther than San Diego Bay to catch a charter boat to a "South of the Border" diving adventure. No California coastal diving experience would be complete without a visit to these three little islands.

1. OSCAR'S HOLE

DEPTH:	20-30 FEET
LEVEL:	NOVICE TO
	INTERMEDIATE

Located at Middle Grounds, Oscar's Hole hosts a veritable geological smorgasbord. Protruding from the cormorant- and pelican-covered shores are a series of finger reefs that create rocky crevices and sand-filled valleys. Visibility can be varied in this region. Its relative open proximity to swells and current can mean clear blue water or a haze of plankton, depending on conditions.

The reef formations are covered with an abundance of orange gorgonian sea fans, patches of purple encrusting corals, and colonies of blue and pink corynactus anemones.

Large calico bass stalk the outer edges of visibility and quantities of blacksmith school in the shallows. Among the rocks themselves, divers will encounter mottled brown and green ling cod, and the well-camouflaged scorpionfish. The ever-present garibaldi are also at home in the Coronados. However, because the garibaldi is not under the benevolent protection of the California State · Department of Fish and Game, they are often taken by Mexican fishermen. Although American divers are not permitted to bring garibaldi back into California waters, it is always a bit paradoxical to see their filleted flanks for sale on the tile slabs at the Ensenada fish market.

2. PUERTO CUEVA LIGHTHOUSE (S)

DEPTH:	10-30 FEET
LEVEL:	NOVICE TO
	INTERMEDIATE

This protected headland at the north end of Coronado del Sur is marked by a lighthouse and often affords a calm harbor in which to anchor and dive. The intertidal zone is a familiar haulout for resident harbor seals that laze about on the dark rocks while relishing the afternoon sun. Good visibility is the norm here, generally averaging in the 30- to 60-foot range, allowing boaters a good view of the terrain and marine life from the surface. Boulders strewn about the base of the cliff create a jumble of interesting terrain and an excellent habitat for marine life. Thick strands of feather-boa kelp grow close to shore. In this feathery undersea garden, schools of Spanish mackerel dart in and out of the stalks, only to explode in retreat when a hungry seal suddenly descends upon them. Other reef residents encountered at this site include calico bass, opaleye and blacksmith.

The boulders give way to sand flats interspersed with thin strands of *Macrocystis* (giant) kelp. In the 30- to 40-foot depths, the terrain becomes relatively barren except for several large plateau-like protrusions that stretch offshore. These formations are dominated by small walls and overhanging crevices.

3. CASINO POINT (S)

DEPTH:	10-40 FEET
LEVEL:	NOVICE TO INTERMEDIATE

Several hundred yards around the corner from Puerto Cueva is a smaller reef-lined cove with another promontory on its southern end. Small shacks and corrugated tin roofs compose the humble dwellings of a small fishing village nestled along the side of the cliffs beside the former casino buildings. Rugged foot trails run up and down the incline of this fishing camp. Lobster trap floats dot the waters inside the cove and around its rocky edges.

Excellent snorkeling. While the casino area makes for great diving, its rocky shallows also offer excellent snorkeling. Here the free diver can swim over wide expanses of undulating eel grass as the bright green strands weave back and forth in the surge. Snorkelers can surface right alongside a suprised harbor seal or a covey of red-beaked black oystercatchers at the water's edge. These small sea birds scurry back and forth along the intertidal zone, picking among the rocks for a meal.

At Casino Point, the reef drops to a bottom of sand and flat rocks in 40 feet of water.

4. THE GAP

DEPTH:	50-75 FEET
LEVEL:	INTERMEDIATE

The Gap is located between Middle Island and Middle Rock. Though an excellent diving area, conditions can be less than ideal since it is completely open to wind, swell and current. However, when conditions are calm, this site offers a superb example of Coronados diving.

Divers will encounter terraced reefs and small seamounts that start at about 50 feet and end in the sand at 75 feet. There is an absence of kelp here, but aquatic visitors will often encounter large bat rays gliding over the sand. Besides white sea urchins, there is little else to be found in the sand.

The main areas of interest at The Gap lie amidst the rocky reef system. Invertebrate life abounds, yet game does not. Fragile, blood and rainbow starfish blanket the rocks, delighting photographers with their tremendous variety of textures and colors. Divers will also find octopus, small scallops, sea palms and numerous gorgonian sea fans. These colorful purple, orange and red fans inundate the bottom terrain. An excellent assortment of corynactus anemones in a variety of hues cover the reefs. Scattered on the reefs are spiny sea urchins and large gray moon sponges. The rock ledges stairstep to the deeper depths, much like Talcott Shoals at Santa Rosa Island, albeit on a smaller scale. The reefs are often interspersed with sandy lanes where bat stars roam.

Like most of the Coronados, the fish encountered are juveniles, as larger specimens are harvested rapidly by local fishermen. The Gap features numerous blacksmith, senorita wrasse and small perch.

5. SEAL COVE

DEPTH:	20-40 FEET
LEVEL:	NOVICE TO INTERMEDIATE

This cove on Middle Island is an excellent last dive of the day due to its diverse terrain and abundant marine life found in shallow water. Usually, there is a bit of surge, but overall the anchorage is well protected. Rocky points at both ends of the cove pierce outward forming small walls with sheer drop-offs. Depths here rarely range beyond 40 feet.

As its name suggests, Seal Cove is home to numerous sea lions and harbor seals. The fanciful sea lions like to play hide and seek with divers, whereas the harbor seals tend to be more shy. The eel grass prevalent in the shallows makes an excellent area for photographing cavorting sea lions.

There is no kelp here save for a few sparse strands staging a comeback. As with most of the Coronados, small cleaner wrasse, garibaldi and blacksmith are plentiful throughout the area.

CHAPTER IV   CORTES BANK

Refer to map on page 22.

Exposed to the raw power of rolling ocean swells, the distant Cortes Bank provides open ocean diving at its best. Depending on one's port of departure, Cortes Bank is 90 to 100 miles out to sea. There are no islands nearby, although on exceptionally clear days one can often catch a fleeting glimpse of San Clemente Island off in the distance. The Bank, a large area that in places rises to within 20 feet of the surface, is marked by only two buoys. Nature's marker, however, is more dramatic for at low tide the reef known as Bishop Rock boils with pounding surf.

HISTORY

Little is known of the early explorers and sailors that passed the treacherous shallows at Cortes Bank. Understandably, most mariners gave the area a wide berth due to its shallow reefs and large surging waves. In 1855 the clipper ship *Bishop* crashed onto Cortes' treacherous shallow boilers and bestowed the name Bishop Rock to its final resting point. Rumors abound that in 1717 a Spanish galleon came to grief on the shoals of Cortes carrying three quarters of a million dollars worth of treasure. No salvagers have yet to locate the galleon's remains.

GEOGRAPHY

Cortes Bank is a huge seamount about 25 miles long and seven miles wide. Local navigation charts consider Cortes to be southern California's farthest outlying coastal danger. The nearest land mass is San Clemente Island, located over 40 miles away.

Access to this lonely ocean outpost should never be taken for granted. A combination of distance and often unfavorable weather protects the pristine conditions at Cortes from becoming overcrowded with divers. Even on the calmest days, a small rolling swell will keep a dive boat bucking at anchor. The continual lurch caused by the Pacific swells contacting the shallow bottom of Cortes tests the sea legs of even veteran divers, often making suiting up a difficult chore.

Calm waters and sunshine can prevail, though conditions can change rapidly when rain squalls blow in. They often leave as quickly as they come. Once out at Cortes, a boat is committed to the open ocean and there is no protection from rough weather should it come. A powerful current can pick up quickly and the fog rolls in unexpectedly at Cortes. Without warning, an increasing wind can raise heavy seas. If you are even remotely prone to seasickness, do yourself a favor and stay at home.

The normal trip to Cortes lasts three days and is for experienced hands only. For those divers willing to challenge the elements at the Bank, a submerged treasure trove waits to be seen.

DIVING CORTES BANK

Cortes Bank is representative of what the marine environment of the southern California coast was like 20 to 30 years ago. The water color is characterized by a vibrant cobalt blue with visibility usually averaging about 60 feet though it sometimes exceeds 100 feet.

Marine life thrives everywhere the photographer points his viewfinder. California brown pelicans skim above waves, while coveys of sea lions raft together in the open water, their fins directed in unison toward the sun as they warm themselves. Having little contact with divers on a regular basis, marine life is easy to approach and photograph.

Cortes Banks lives up to its reputation as this diver prepares to "bag" a large California spiny lobster.

Recovering from the ravages of fierce storms, thin strands of kelp are staging a comeback in the area. Large rock scallops with gray or orange mantles hide within the brilliant camouflage of canyons and crevices. Pacific electric rays cruise the sandy passages between reefs. Vertical walls are covered with a thick matting of gorgonian fans and bright purple and vermillion Spanish shawl nudibranchs.

One of the special attractions are the varieties of iridescent red hydrocorals that flourish among the walls and ledges throughout the reef system. Cortes also has quite a reputation for large California spiny lobsters with eight to twelve pounders caught regularly.

6. BLUE HORIZONS

DEPTH:	30-130+ FEET
LEVEL:	EXPERIENCED

There is an extensive choice of dive sites at Cortes, most of which are recognized only by Loran numbers. Diving is predominately in the 40- to 80-foot range, but there are equally excellent spots much deeper. When calm, Cortes extends a gracious yet dynamic welcome to those who visit.

By jumping out towards the horizon into the cobalt-blue water, divers will enter a world of canyons, corals, nudibranchs and occasional caverns. Even on the calmest days, there is a constant surge on the bottom. Here, divers are suspended, moving to and fro with the heartbeat of the ocean surge. Graceful sea palms sway in the ebb and flow. Eel and surf grass roll back and forth in an unending curtain call, occasionally revealing a bright red spiny lobster on stage. Schools of Spanish mackerel dance their way through the juvenile kelp strands.

It doesn't take long for an experienced diver to acclimate and feel very much at home at Cortes. Large bull sea lions chase after crowds of bait, attempting to nab an early morning snack. Oversized sheepshead and bass cruise the deep water shadows at the base of the reefs where rocky substrate gives way to coarse white sand.

On the shallower reefs are endless mazes of canyons and crevices. Starting in 60 to 70 feet of water, these systems carve their way through the reef tops and progress upward to the 30- to 40-foot mark. Even when the reef tops are in very shallow water, divers can avoid the tumultuous surge overhead by hugging the bottom of the canyons.

Sinkholes and chimney chutes. On the tops of the reefs, amidst the sway of eel grass, are small sinkholes and chimney chutes that burrow down into the reef, creating protected pockets of calm water. The sinkholes are large and rounded, occasionally as deep as 15 feet. The chimney chutes are tight spheres that are three to five feet in diameter and depth. These calm-water holes are often landscaped by a barrage of sea palms on top, and a plethora of invertebrates inside. Varieties of delicate hydrocorals, anemones and nudibranchs are often found inside these depressions. Occasionally, divers will encounter "bull rings"—sinkholes jam packed with dozens of 6- to 12-pound lobsters. Needless to say, such discoveries cause no small excitement among divers.

Photo tips. Camera enthusiasts will find tremendous photographic opportunites. The ever-present herd of sea lions and the clear, azure water, make for productive sessions with a wide-angle lens. Macro afficionados will find an ever-present array of targets such as nudibranchs, sea stars, corals, snails and anemones. While Cortes has a much deserved reputation for good hunting, few realize that superb photo opportunities abound.

7. THE *ABALONIA*

DEPTH:	30 FEET
LENGTH:	200+ FEET
TYPE:	CEMENT FREIGHTER
LEVEL:	ADVANCED

During periods of swell and low tide, huge breakers pound the angry shallows of Bishop Rock. It is here, in 30 feet of water, that the *Abalonia*, a war surplus cargo ship built of cement, foundered over 25 years ago.

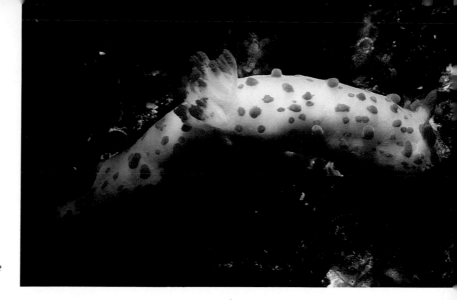

Colorful nudibranchs abound in California waters. This one is the spotted clown.

Caution. When the sea is calm and the tide high, the wreck can be dived, although extreme caution should be used. Powerful suction can pull divers inside the wreck with little warning, smashing them against concrete bulkheads. As the ship lies on its side and continues to break up, the concrete is deteriorating revealing a potentially lethal arsenal of rusting iron reinforcement bars. These long slivers of jagged metal can easily puncture an exposure suit, as well as the diver wearing it. If one is not accustomed to wreck diving in heavy surge, this is definitely not the place to get initiated.

Despite the difficulty of diving the *Abalonia*, the rewards are many. Visibility is usually quite good, and there is a lot left of this large ship to explore. When surge is timed properly, an experienced wreck diver with lights can enter the vessel during a slack period and access its interior. Deep inside the wreck, and far away from the entrance points, the water is virtually still and clear, simulating conditions found in fresh water springs and caves. Bulkheads often house a large contingent of lobster, making it an easy task to bag a day's limit in a single dive.

Caution. Several interior compartments have air pockets where divers can surface. Do not breathe from these pockets! Air pockets inside shipwrecks are not always a source of fresh, breathable air and could prove harmful.

A ladder inside the Abalonia *wreck points to the clear blue waters of Cortes Banks.*

CHAPTER V   SAN NICOLAS ISLAND

Refer to map on page 23.

Sixty-one miles from the coast of southern California lies the remote outpost of San Nicolas Island, the last territorial bastion of the United States before Hawaii.

San Nick, as she is known by many, is U.S. Navy territory and houses approximately 200 military and civilian personnel. A tour of duty at remote San Nicolas qualifies as Navy sea time although the base has been made as comfortable as possible with a housing and business district, a Navy Exchange, a recreational center and a microwave telephone service to the mainland.

The Navy uses the island for gathering data on missile firings into the Pacific Missile Test Range. The island's value to the Navy is obvious, but there are other groups who use the island's environs.

For years, San Nicolas Island has been well known for its numerous marine resources. The waters surrounding the island are a prime producer of the commercial red abalone and sea urchins. The sea urchin market flourishes primarily as an export commodity, sending the roe to Japan where it is highly prized as a delicacy.

Landing access on the island is restricted and boats are required to remain 300 yards offshore. Over the past years, however, this regulation was enforced sporadically, or was applied only to specific areas. Sport fishing and diving vessels would often sneak into these restricted areas for a chance at some rockfish, lobster or abalone. Today the Navy tends to be more vigilant because of a recent controversy.

Lately, another group—The U.S. Fish and Wildlife Service—has cast a covetous eye upon San Nicolas Island. For the past several years, the FWS has pursued San Nicolas as a translocation site for a breeding colony of sea otters. Environmental groups have expressed concern that the northern sea otter colony near Big Sur is threatened by the possibility of an oil spill. Otter advocates maintain that a transplanted second colony in southern California is neccessary in case any harm befalls the northern group. The Fish and Wildlife Service wanted to make San Nicolas a new site to locate a breeding colony of sea otters.

At the end of a long battle involving the commercial shellfish industry, environmental groups, sport divers, the Navy, oil companies and the Department of the Interior, the plan won approval and the transplanting of sea otters began. The Navy again began enforcing its 300-yard limit, making sport diver access to San Nicolas Island more restricted. But dive boat operators still have windows of opportunity when the Navy grants access to some sites on a trip by trip basis.

San Nicolas receives its share of weather especially on the seaward side which is exposed to the full force of swell and wind. Fourteen-knot breezes are the daily norm at San Nick. Gale force northwesterlies are not uncommon. Like a frantic artist, the winds create shifting sand dunes that aimlessly roam about the island. Incessant seas continually carve and reshape the sandstone rock formations within the intertidal zone, battering the headlands with unchecked surf. Windswept, exposed and barren, San Nicolas is a desert far out at sea, but has an oasis of life submerged beneath her waters.

HISTORY

California's aboriginal Indians inhabited San Nicolas Island until the arrival of the European explorers and the establishment of the church missions. The natives that populated the island

The Spanish shawl is one of the most striking varieties of nudibranchs.

Fun-loving sea lions are often encountered in the waters of San Nicolas Island.

were called Nicolenos; a culturally distinct group of island-dwelling Indians as compared to the mainland Chumash and Gabrielino. The Nicolenos were artisans, carving petroglyphs of killer whales on sandstone walls of caves, creating ornate bowls and vessels, and carving bone and wood sculptures. Like other tribes found off the California coast, the Nicolenos were a gathering and fishing group who occasionally hunted the numerous sea lions and fur seals found along the island's shores.

Sailing southward after the death of Juan Cabrillo in 1543, Bartolome Ferrer passed San Nicolas Island and noted its position on his charts. Little else is known of other early visitors.

In the early 1800's, Yankee otter hunters filled the history books with tales of ravage and slaughter.

Following the example of Russian trappers, the Americans imported Kodiak and Aleutian hunters from the far northwest to assist in obtaining otter skins. These well-armed hunters were dropped off on various islands for hunting purposes, and picked up later. At San

Nicolas, the Kodiak hunters raped the Nicoleno women and handily killed the males who came to their rescue. At one time, San Nicolas had a population of over 1,000 Indians and an abundance of sea otter. With the coming of the Kodiaks and Aleuts in 1811, both sea otter and Nicoleno populations were slaughtered to near extermination.

In 1835, Catholic priests from the San Gabriel Mission chartered a vessel to bring the remaining Indians to the mainland for protection.

With the Indians removed, San Nicolas Island became home to squatter camps of Japanese and Chinese fishermen, and ranchers of sheep, cattle and horses. During World War II, San Nicolas fell under Army jurisdiction where it served as a bombing and artillery range. At the close of the war, the island became permanent property of the U.S. Navy, who divided it into three zones, Alpha, Bravo and Charlie.

GEOGRAPHY

San Nicolas is the fifth largest island off the California coast, and is noted particularly for its rocky beaches and offshore sandspits. The island's topography is mesa-like with the

The Lone Woman of San Nicolas

In the 1920's, Scott O'Dell wrote his famous book, the Island of the Blue Dolphins. Although his work was fiction, it was based on the Indians remaining on San Nicolas.

The island population was decimated by Kodiak otter hunters dropped off on the island by Yankee and Russian fur traders in the early 1800's. The Kodiaks ravished Nicoleno women, killed most of the men, and decimated the sea otter population. Prior to this, it is estimated that as many as 1,000 Nicolenos lived on the island.

In 1835, Franciscan Mission Fathers removed the remaining Nicolenos to the mainland for their protection. One woman did not leave on the Mexican schooner. Realizing that her child was not in the group, she dove over the side of the ship and swam to shore as the anchor was being raised. The ship did not return for her. Her child had been killed by wild dogs by the time she swam back to the shore.

Eighteen years later, California pioneer and adventurer Captain George Nidever visited the island and brought the woman back to Santa Barbara. She lived with Nidever and his family for six weeks. Unaccustomed to mainland life, she died shortly thereafter. Before her death, she was baptized "Juana Maria." She is buried in the Santa Barbara Mission cemetery.

During the years she lived alone on San Nicolas Island, she existed on shellfish, sea lions, wild roots and sea birds. Her dwelling was made of whale ribs, sea lion hides and brush.

highest elevation just over 900 feet. Composed primarily of sandstone, San Nicolas bears the characteristics of other neighboring islands with sand dunes, badlands and marine terraces.

Like San Miguel, San Nicolas has caliche deposits. These eerie limestone casings of ancient plant life leave a spectral legacy of the primitive trees that once flourished on the island. Today, San Nick is covered with patches of yellow coreopsis flowers, buckwheat and poison oak. During the late 60's, specimens of mainland trees and shrubs were introduced to the island in an attempt to overcome its sparse appearance.

DIVING

San Nicolas' apparent desolation stops abruptly at the waterline. The intertidal zone is a haul out for fur seals, elephant seals and California sea lions, and sustains a healthy population of waterfowl. Venturing farther from the surf-pounded rocks at the waterline, divers quickly discover that a very dynamic habitat awaits them.

Visibility is not always on a tropical scale, hence San Nick is known best for its game, rather than scenic opportunities. However, San Nicolas does have its photogenic qualities, and is visited for more than just hunting forays.

Yet, it is for good reason that San Nick is most often visited by divers during lobster season. Over the years, San Nicolas Island has developed a reputation as "Land of the Giants." Big 6- to 10-pound lobsters are the rule rather than the exception. Of course, diving San Nick does not guarantee that a diver will bring home a limit of gargantuan crustaceans. Sometimes, even the best hunters will return to the boat with an empty game bag. San Nicolas is also an excellent producer

The big lobsters of San Nicolas Island are a much sought after prize of bug hunters.

The sea urchin's roe is considered a delicacy in Japan. They are commercially harvested in the waters surrounding San Nicolas Island.

Strong currents and open ocean swells sweep through the area at times, making diving there a rare commodity. On those marginal days, most dive boats tuck into the rock's lee, which affords some protection from crashing waves. During conditions such as these, divers quickly jump into the water, make a single dive and then retreat to San Nicolas. But when divers can approach the area on one of those legendary calm days, it is possible to spend the entire day at Begg Rock.

Unless plankton blooms are present, visibility is usually phenomenal. The reef system consists of three main pinnacles and a shallow razorback ridge connecting two of them. Hundreds of feet of water drop between the pinnacles, but the excellent visibility permits divers to traverse the expanse of blue water and swim from peak to peak. Diving at Begg Rock can range from 20- to 30-foot shallows to extreme depths.

Tapestries of starfish. Pancake-size scallops grow along the ledges as do myriads of anemone colonies. A diver swimming over the checkerboard distinctions of anemone fields can liken the experience to flying over farmlands in a commercial airplane. Each separate specie of anemone appears to congregate on clearly defined plots of reef. The same is true with vast massings of starfish. The sheer volcanic walls at Begg Rock have wall-to-wall living tapestries of bat stars, giant green stars, fragile rainbow stars and others. These colorful quilts are in patterns of green, purple, yellow, lavender, orange, cobalt blue and red.

Caution. Due to the great depths divers can potentially attain, one must pay constant attention to depth gauges at Begg Rock. During calm periods, repetitive dives can be made, but as always, careful pre-dive planning must be made.

13. ALPHA FOUL AREA

DEPTH:	12-60+ FEET
LEVEL:	EXPERIENCED

When the Navy grants access to this area, it usually produces an excellent lobster catch. During low tide, the shallow portions of this site are awash with white water breakers.

Divers working the seaward side of the Foul Area will find depths in the mid-30's range and a terrain of many shallow crevices. If lobster are inhabiting these holes, it is an easy task to pull them out since they have no escape. The seabed is relatively barren with sparse kelp and a multitude of purple sea urchins. Towards the end of the season, lobsters gravitate more in the shallower water at this site and lobster grabbers can do quite well for themselves.

Caution. Watch out for strong surge in the shallows, especially during low tide and periods of swell.

14. CHARLIE AREA SANDSPIT

DEPTH:	15-60 FEET
LEVEL:	INTERMEDIATE TO EXPERIENCED

Mariners should be wary approaching this area. Shifting sand shoals and breaking waves often result in dangerous conditions while crossing near the southeast corner of the island. Many boats however, will anchor for the evening slightly south of the sandspit when the wind is not blowing.

Here, kelp grows on top of several small low-lying finger reefs. Interestingly, these shallow reefs produce large lobster in small holes—a bug grabber's dream!

Due to the usual inhospitable conditions, the sandspit is not often dived. The low-lying sand dunes on shore deflect the average 15 to 25 knot wind off the island and directly into the area, making it difficult for a boat's anchor to hold unless it is hooked fast onto a rock. When conditions are right however, charter boats do well in this area.

CHAPTER **VI** SAN CLEMENTE ISLAND

Refer to map on page 24.

San Clemente is often considered "The Summertime Island." Although excellent diving is available year round, the best weather is from May through October when sunny skies prevail and winds are fair.

San Clemente Island is located 41 miles off the southern California coast, and 21 miles from Catalina Island. The island is large enough to provide ample protected anchorages.

Like other offshore islands in the Peninsular Range, San Clemente is inhabited and controlled by the military. The Northwest Harbor facility is home to S.E.A.L. and U.D.T. teams from the Naval Underwater Warfare Unit. The remaining portion of the island is used as an artillery and bombing range. At evening's anchorage, many a dive boat has received a free airshow, as Navy F14s and A4s play "Topgun" along the island's backside. At a safe distance, divers can watch jets drop live payloads on nearby beaches, pillboxes and dummy tanks.

One should not feel deterred in visiting San Clemente for fear of taking an active role in peacetime live fire exercises. Portions of the island are periodically closed, but these closures are posted weekly in the Notice to Mariners report issued by the U.S. Coast Guard. Civilian access to the island itself is prohibited. Even though part of the island's waters may be closed at times, there is usually a good selection of excellent areas to dive.

HISTORY

The first European to see San Clemente Island was the intrepid Portuguese navigator Juan Rodríguez Cabrillo. He sailed past the island in 1542, but records do not indicate that a landing party went ashore. San Clemente received its name in 1602 from Sebastian Vizcaino who also passed without stopping. In 1769, the Spaniard Gasparde Portola's expedition landed at Pyramid Cove and was greeted by gift-bearing natives. The Indians called the island Kinkipar.

Evidence suggests that a significant Indian population once inhabited the island. Historians believe these Indians were probably Gabrielinos who lived off the sea. While details of Indian life on San Clemente remain sketchy, it is believed that the occupants abandoned their homes for the mainland before 1830. Occasionally, fragments of stone bowls and other implements are discovered underwater at San Clemente.

After the Indians, various fishermen, whalers and hunters occupied the island prior to the turn of the century. Government leases were later granted for sheep, goat and cattle grazing. Spartan ranch and bunkhouse facilities were built at Wilson Cove. At the height of this enterprise, more than 11,000 sheep grazed on the island, heavily impacting its ecology. The ranching period ended with the onset of World War II when the island came under military jurisdiction. Today the sheep are gone. The wild goats have been scheduled for eradication, but for the moment, protests from environmental groups have halted large scale culling.

GEOGRAPHY

San Clemente Island is an area of extreme geological diversity that begins above its shores and descends far beneath the waterline. Relatively long and narrow, this 21-mile long island varies in width between two and four miles. The leeward side of the island features

Perhaps no scene is as representative of California diving as a garibaldi among the kelp fronds.

precipitous cliffs with jagged caverns carved along its face that plunge into the sea. On the exposed western portion of the island well-defined terraces end in sandy beaches.

San Clemente is largely composed of volcanic and sedimentary rock, much of which is sandstone. The combination has resulted in some interesting terrain that ranges from rolling grassy hills and scrub brush to barren primordial rockscapes.

DIVING

The underwater caverns, canyons, walls, ledges and reef systems are all teeming with a plethora of colorful marine life.

Water clarity ranges from 60 to 100 feet, depending on which site you choose to visit. Areas where white sand bottoms are fringed with reefs and kelp generally have the best visibility. The white sand is reflective and bounces back ambient rays, bathing the surrounding area in a flood of diffused light.

For the hunter seeking varieties of game, San Clemente has a lot to offer. From May through

July, yellowtail and halibut are running. It is not uncommon for a well-versed breath hold diver to snorkel out into blue water and encounter a silvery boil of hundreds of large pelagic jack swirling about. In general, shooting the fish is easy compared to selecting which fish to shoot as the solid wall of reflected silver passes by.

Abalone and lobster are always available for the sea going gourmet, but remember to follow all current California Fish and Game laws. More than once, a Fish and Game representative has boarded a boat while divers were underwater and waited by the dive ladder with citation book in hand. Fines are expensive.

San Clemente really shines for the photographer, specifically those using a wide-angle system. Clear water results in superb shooting conditions. Thick, opulent kelp canopies converge on the surface of sheltered coves. Amber and emerald rays of light diffuse through the foilage to create a breathtaking underwater cathedral.

Divers swimming beneath ledges will encounter shafts of light bouncing on colorful gorgonians which give even the most well-traveled divers a feeling of reverence and awe.

The reefs provide a habitat for colorful moon snails, pink and purple sea fans with extended polyps, and schools of jack mackerel. These treasures and more provide enough subject material to exhaust a roll of film in short order.

15. PYRAMID COVE

DEPTH:	15-80+ FEET
LEVEL:	INTERMEDIATE TO EXPERIENCED

Contrary to popular belief, the Pyramid Cove area is not just an anchorage where all diving and fishing boats congregate when the weather turns foul. True, the orientation of the headlands offers excellent protection from the

A natural sculpture of driftwood adorns one of San Clemente's rocky beaches. Photo: Courtesy of the National Park Service.

Tube anemones are delicate creatures and should only be observed and photographed.

A silver perch among the kelp at San Clemente Island.

wilds of wind and wave, but there is more here than a safe haven for boaters.

Pyramid Cove is located at the extreme southeast end of San Clemente where the windward and leeward corners of the island meet. The result is interesting terrain both above and beneath the surface. A towering bluff slopes downward into a rocky "Y" shaped bight. This craggy and desolate area hosts little surface vegetation. The moon-like landscape features several interesting terrestrial formations, one of which is a pyramid-shaped mound near the windward side of the island— hence the name "Pyramid Cove" or "Pyramid Head." This natural anchorage features a thick bed of kelp throughout its environs, thinning out where the rocks give way to a sand bottom in 70 to 80 feet of water.

Visibility at Pyramid varies depending on conditions. When calm seas prevail and southerly swells do not, the surface water resembles a mirrored lake. Sunlight bounces off the kelp canopy transforming the entire

cove into a sea of amber with clear blue patches of open water for divers to descend through. When the backside of the island receives its share of incoming swell, Pyramid is often the last area to be affected, and can still remain an excellent dive. Even when clarity is reduced to an "unbearable" 30 feet, diving is still good.

Bull calicos. Beneath the kelp canopy is a variety of terrain and marine life. Along the inshore shallows, the bottom is relatively flat. Crevices and ledges are hidden by sheets of green eel grass that undulate softly in the surge. Frightened calico bass will explode out of their camouflaged lairs and head for open water. The accurate bass hunter can do well here as San Clemente is known for its 7- to 10-pound "bull" calicos. This area is also resplendent with sea palms, garibaldi and a variety of sea urchins. Kelp is thick in the shallows. If working into these areas, be sure to save enough air to navigate back to the boat beneath the kelp canopy. This helps divers large and short, about 40 to 50 feet in length. A dive light is not necessary, but will highlight details making the dive more interesting. Gorgonian fans grace the ceiling and walls, and small lobsters are almost always tucked into the higher crevices.

Divers opting to pass on venturing inside the cavern system will enjoy visiting the lush kelp beds on the outside. Visibility averages only about 20 feet because the site is on the west side of the island. When swells are not present, water clarity can improve to 40 feet and beyond.

21. NINE FATHOM

DEPTH:	55-90 FEET
LEVEL:	INTERMEDIATE TO EXPERIENCED

Nine Fathom is a popular site on the northwest corner of the island near Castle Rock. There is no protection from incoming swells here so the boat tends to wallow in the trough—something to consider if you are prone to seasickness. Although there is usually surge present, it is Nine Fathom's open-ocean environment that is responsible for its interesting aquatic features.

The currents that often roar through the site help maintain the excellent water clarity. Visibility is usually in the 60- to 120-foot range, but occasionally is even better.

In the 55- to 90-foot range, divers will encounter bright concentrations of red and purple hydrocorals. Resembling a shorter version of elkhorn coral found in the Caribbean, these colorful hydrocorals are exceptionally beautiful. To view fully their vividness, bring along a dive light. When bathed in artificial light, a transformation occurs and the dull blue color bursts into vibrantly warm hues. Rich red, orange and purple gorgonians also abound.

A small amount of kelp grows in the area as compared to other sites on the island. Large bass and pelagic jacks cruise by. Occasional ocean sunfish are also seen.

22. WINDOWPANE

DEPTH:	60-110+ FEET
LEVEL:	EXPERIENCED

Windowpane is an intense and dramatic blue-water dive. It is deep; the top of the reef jutts out from the nearby shore and then takes an abrupt drop at the 40-foot mark quickly plummeting beyond 110 feet. There is little bottom sediment here. On a sunny day with calm water and a mild current, visibility can be excellent. It is not uncommon for a photographer at 60 feet to frame a large pink gorgonian and still capture the silhouette of the dive boat.

Moray eels. Flourishing on the face of the drop-off are budding branches of pink, orange and red gorgonian fans, as well as yellow aggregating anemones, all fed by prevailing current. At deeper depths are numerous crevices that house a stable colony of moray eels. Although these snaggle-toothed reef residents will never win any beauty contests, they are docile and harmless. The eels come in a variety of sizes; a great convenience considering not all extension tubes are created equal. If your model is too large or too small, simply swim over to the next crevice and find the one that best suits your framer or lens.

At Windowpane, the deeper one descends, the better the diving becomes. The wall eventually transforms into a bottom of rocky rubble interspersed with sand.

Caution. Don't let the deceptive beauty of Windowpane's wall captivate you for too long. Due to the depth involved, decompression limits are reached quickly. Watch your computer or follow dive tables conservatively and be sure to monitor your air supply.

This 20-pound yellowtail was speared while free-diving in the waters surrounding San Clemente.

23. LITTLE FLOWER

DEPTH:	30-75 FEET
LEVEL:	NOVICE TO INTERMEDIATE

Very close to Windowpane is a smaller, yet no less spectacular wall known as Little Flower. The terrain on the extreme northern end of this site is similar to Windowpane—steep and deep. The southern side, however, ambles into a shallow series of ledges that provide options for those not wanting to make a deep dive. This side features an underwater landslide of small boulders that cascade to the sand bottom at 75 feet. The water here is usually very still, blue and quiet so visibility often exceeds 100 feet.

Little Flower is a migrating point for yellowtail jack that circle the island in the summer months pursuing baitfish. These larger pelagic fish generally scatter (although not always) at the sound of regulator exhaust bubbles. However, for the free diver without scuba, a special experience is often reserved. When free diving during periods of migration, the diver can be caught in the melee as a solid wall of fish weaves around him. The area suddenly explodes in a quicksilver flash of brilliance as 15- to 30-pound yellowtail blast through the water like agile jet fighters.

Spearfishing. Some free divers bring specially rigged spear guns into the water while in pursuit of large game fish. These guns are long and feature heavy shafts with breakway points. They are often rigged with a quick release and 100 feet of polypropylene line attached to a trailing Norwegian buoy on the surface. This allows the free diver to shoot the fish (perhaps at a depth of 40 to 60 feet) and swim back to the surface for a breath of air.

The old time blue water hunters will wrestle the struggling giant back to the surface without the use of a float. Unfortunately, very few of these living legends are around today.

Even if you are just swimming with these magnificent fish, or stalking them with a camera, the experience is incredible. If the yellowtail, bonita, or bluefin don't happen to cross your path, the mackerel usually do. These billowing clouds of bait are encountered in the Little Flower area during warmer summer months.

Little Flower's shallows host an undersea garden of eel grass and sea palms. This is often a treasure trove of large calico bass, lurking deceptively among the rock piles, taking advantage of the additional camouflage. Some of these bass are quite old and run into the 10-pound range, offering additional challenges for the underwater hunter. The bass, however, seem to understand the difference between a camera and spear gun. Consequently, photographers can get quite close; hunters experience greater difficulty.

On the outside ledge, Little Flower hosts gorgonians, fiesty garibaldis and moray eels. Although the drop-off is not as dramatic as Windowpane's, Little Flower is still a dive with much to offer. With the shallower depths found here, it's a great last dive of the day when residual nitrogen restricts available bottom time.

CHAPTER VII   SANTA CATALINA ISLAND

Refer to map on page 24.

Santa Catalina is one of southern California's most readily accessible islands, yet it is often overlooked. Located 20 miles offshore across the Catalina Channel, this large land mass is close to the major dive boat ports of San Pedro and Long Beach. It takes only two hours to arrive by charter boat and less by private speedboat.

The majority of the island's rugged coastline conceals a wealth of excellent diving areas, yet Catalina is often dubbed the "checkout island."

While it is true that many West Coast divers receive their first taste of the underwater world at Catalina Island, they rarely return to explore the island further. There is, however, more diving adventure available here than meets the eye, and only a short boat ride from home.

HISTORY

The best known early inhabitants of Catalina Island were the Gabrielino Indians. In 1542, when Juan Rodríguez Cabrillo's exploratory caravels sailed up the California coast, there were hundreds of tribesmen living in villages scattered across the island. They were friendly to the Spaniards.

Cabrillo originally named the island San Salvador. However, it was the intrepid merchant-explorer Sebastian Vizcaino who received the final credit of bestowing the island's permanent name, Santa Catalina, in honor of Saint Catherine.

Unfortunately, the fate of the Gabrielinos was sealed with the arrival of the European explorers. As on most of California's offshore islands, the Indian population declined with the coming of the Spaniards and their missions, and the arrival of Russian and Yankee otter hunters. Exploited and abused in later years by these visitors, the Gabrielinos were eventually assimilated into mission culture on the mainland. They finally faded into obscurity as the indigenous race vanished.

After the decline of Spanish influence, Alta California and its offshore islands were ceded to Mexico. During this period of government, Catalina Island was granted to Thomas Robbins. Robbins later sold his interest, and a variety of proprietorships ensued, including military possession by the Fourth Infantry of California Volunteers during the Civil War. The island later became owned by entrepreneur George Shatto who paid $200,000 for it in 1887.

It was Shatto who began building the town of Avalon that was named after the Tennyson poem, "Idylls of the King." Avalon quickly developed as a summer resort destination. Tents gave way to cottages, and eventually, the grand Hotel Metropole was built. Later, Shatto went broke and William Wrigley purchased complete interest in the island. During the Wrigley years, the famed Avalon casino was built and tourism was promoted heavily. Big band concerts performed regularly on the island. In the 1920's and 30's, Avalon became a favorite hideaway for the wealthy of Los Angeles and revelers cruised the Channel in white steamships heading for Catalina's idyllic shores. After World War II Avalon's attractiveness began to fade. The grand steamships, *Avalon* and *Catalina* retired from service and small, swift water taxis took over.

GEOGRAPHY

Santa Catalina, the third largest of the Channel Islands group, is rivaled only by her northern sisters, Santa Cruz and Santa Rosa. Characterized by steep, rugged mountains and hillside canyons, the terrain on Catalina Island is often formidable; well suited to the

A wreck dive, complete with a background of kelp, is only one of the highlights of Avalon's Underwater Park.

mountain goats, buffalo and bald eagles that reside there. Along the island's 54 miles of coastline are certain areas where these vertical features give way to sloping sandy beaches and protected coves. This low-lying relief is only temporary for a few hundred yards to either end of the beaches, the terrain rises again to the volcanic cliffs that plunge into the sea. The island's interior is very different and consists of hills and valleys, with rolling green grasslands, oak woodlands, scrub brush and chaparral.

DIVING

At Catalina, divers will discover much more than the patch of sand where they completed their certification skills. There are varieties of walls, sheer drop-offs, ledges, rolling reefs and caverns for divers to swim through and explore. Thick kelp rings many of the island's coves creating, on sunny days, a surrealistic amber forest splashed with highlights of green and yellow.

As for marine life, divers will encounter everything from nudibranchs and tube anemones to Pacific electric rays, yellowtails, and an occassional blue shark.

26. LITTLE FARNSWORTH

DEPTH:	40-90 FEET
LEVEL:	EXPERIENCED

Few commercial dive boats visit this obscure spot a few minutes' boat ride east of Avalon. Little Farnsworth is an offshore highspot that rises to within 50 feet of the surface and drops into the sand below at 90 feet. The sand slopes off into deeper water.

The area is relatively pristine. Large scallops line the rocks, and incredible varieties of corals branch off the walls as the terrain cascades vertically in a system of canyons, walls and crevices. Underneath ledges, an occasional large lobster can be found—rare for the overfished lee side of Catalina Island. Visibility is variable depending on plankton levels, swell and current, but as a rule, the east end of the island near Avalon features excellent water clarity.

27. AVALON'S UNDERWATER PARK (S)

DEPTH:	20-90 FEET
LEVEL:	NOVICE TO
	INTERMEDIATE

Divers will quickly find that the nearby Avalon's Underwater Park off Casino Point offers visitors numerous aquatic options. A variety of geological terrain such as drop-offs, steep ledges and rocky reefs can be found here. Depths range from shallow recesses to beyond 100 feet. Several shipwrecks rest within the Park's boundaries, including a 65-foot sailboat. Dense kelp grows off the breakwater protecting Avalon Harbor. Local fish seem to be aware that the Park is a marine preserve as large bass, lobster, eel and other marine critters are easily approached by divers. Visibility is usually in the 60- to 100-foot range.

The Park boundary begins in front of the breakwater and extends beyond the casino. The Park itself is roped off to boat traffic, allowing aquatic explorers the opportunity to relax and concentrate on diving rather than the boats thundering in and out of the Harbor. All diving at the Park is accessed from the rocks in front of the casino. Boat divers can visit the Park by anchoring outside the roped buoys and swimming in.

The extreme southeastern boundary of the Park is the breakwater itself. This area quickly drops to 90 feet and is where the wreck of the sailboat *Sue Jac* is located. A thick bed of kelp normally covers this area.

Closer to the casino, the terrain changes from a steep slope to a gradual drop-off. Barrel Roll, Hammerhead, Many Rock, and Moray are rock formations that rise near the surface from 35- to 50-foot depths, creating small walls and drop-offs. Divers will encounter multicolored gorgonians, Christmas tree worms, garibaldi, bass, sheepshead, senorita, blacksmith and rock wrasse in these areas. Kelp is not as thick as on the breakwater, affording an abundance of wide open terrain. Here, almost tame lobsters and eels await the photographer.

Man-made habitats. Moving to the Park's northern boundary near Descanso Bay, divers will find many man-made habitats and some small wrecks. These wrecks consist of an underwater junkyard of pontoon boats, fishing boats, dock material and other derelict items submerged intentionally to attract fish for the enjoyment of divers. In this area is a rubber tire habitat. This circular jungle provides shelter for invertebrates; there's usually an octopus or two setting up house. A sunken automobile nearby functions in the same capacity. To reach this area, it is necessary to navigate out of the Park boundaries into deeper water. Be sure to save enough air to return underwater to avoid the boat traffic.

On weekends and during the summer, you'll find many divers enjoying the Underwater Park. While the breakwater and seawall may be crowded at times, the underwater part of the Park is large enough to accommodate all. During the summer, from Fridays through Saturdays, the Catalina Divers' Supply air truck is stationed at the Park to provide airfills. At midweek, the Park is relatively uncrowded, and in the winter, the site is almost deserted.

Note. There is no hunting or collecting permitted in the Park.

28. LONG POINT (S)

DEPTH:	20-60 FEET
LEVEL:	INTERMEDIATE

There is a good dive at Catalina's Long Point as well as an excellent anchorage for protection from afternoon winds. Just a short distance from Avalon, this site features varied terrain including sand, large crevices, overhangs, finger reefs and shallow water drop-offs. Depths average between 20 and 60 feet with rocks giving way to sand at the base of the reef. The shallows offer interesting diving in patches of eel grass undulating in the surge. The usual complement of Catalina sea creatures are always present. During spring and summer months, divers may be treated to an underwater traffic jam of hundreds of swirling mackerel.

29. HEN ROCK (S)

DEPTH:	20-40 FEET
LEVEL:	NOVICE

This site is very close to Long Point, but is protected by headlands and cliffs, and thus offers a greater degree of shelter from the wind. Hen Rock's placid waters make an excellent choice for a night boat dive. Fortunate divers may find lobsters walking about in the open. This is also a good area for observing large moray eels among the rock piles and crevices. Visibility averages 30 to 40 feet. The maximum depth here is about 40 feet.

A variety of features including ledges, drop-offs and shipwrecks are available at Avalon's Underwater Park. Some of the dive sites are roped off to protect divers from boat traffic.

Sea lions can often be seen on rock formations at the east end of Catalina.

30. YELLOWTAIL POINT

DEPTH:	40-90+ FEET
LEVEL:	INTERMEDIATE TO EXPERIENCED

Yellowtail Point has terrain that is quite unique. A reef of jumbled rocks protrudes seaward and then turns parallel to shore. The main section of the reef is in 40 to 50 feet of water but a diver can follow the reef until it meets the sand in 90 feet of water. The sand continues to slope into deeper depths.

Yellowtail Point can be an excellent producer of lobster, but be aware that the same crevice that offers a potential dinner usually houses a moray eel. Gorgonians thrive on the boulders as do starfish and varieties of anemones. Yellowtail Point is a prolific site for photographers, but visibility rarely exceeds 30 feet.

31. ROCKY QUARRY AREA (S)

DEPTH:	20-130 FEET
LEVEL:	NOVICE TO EXPERIENCED

The Rock Quarry Area is located east of the Isthmus and Blue Cavern Point. Its high, protective cliffs offer boaters excellent protection from prevailing afternoon winds.

Rocky promontories ring the edge of this small bay and provide protection from currents that pick up in many other areas on the island. It is a wide area with a breakwater-type point made of quarry stone flanking its eastern corner.

Excellent diving is found within the thick surrounding kelp bed. Sheer cliffs ring the extreme eastern end, and a sandy beach sits in the middle of the cove. Generally, the flattest, calmest water on the island is found in the Rock Quarry Area.

To the west of the cove's center is a small series of white rocks that branch out from the intertidal area at the base of a steep cliff. Here, kelp grows thickly a short distance from shore. The real attraction, however, is in 20 feet of water where a cavern system opens at the front of a wall. The interior of the cavern is adorned with a bouquet of red, yellow and purple gorgonian fans. To the rear of the cavern, which penetrates approximately 25 feet, several crevices and chutes bring in shafts of light, adding an ethereal glow to the interior. Inside the cavern calico bass hover motionless in a semi-suspended state and sleeping swell sharks doze beneath the overhangs in the rear. Though ambient light is everywhere, dive lights will bring out the brillance of the gorgonian corals. The interior is large and roomy and divers are never far from exit points. The cavern at white rocks is probably one of Catalina's most picturesque and tranquil dives.

32. SHIP ROCK

DEPTH:	30-130 FEET
LEVEL:	INTERMEDIATE TO EXPERIENCED

Without a doubt, Ship Rock is one of the best dives on the lee side of Catalina Island. In the fall and late summer months, visibility can exceed the 130-foot mark. Ship Rock is a marine seamount that breaks the surface. It resembles a guano-covered Matterhorn 60 feet high. Below the waterline its slopes hide a vast resource of aquatic treasures. This underwater skyscraper bottoms out in the sand at 130 feet. Depending on the dive boat's approach, which is influenced by wind and current conditions, the drop-off can be a steep precipice or a rolling razorback that plummets sharply on each side. This is a good deep dive, but there is plenty to see for the diver that chooses to remain at shallower depths.

At certain times of the year along the deep water sand plains are dozens of 4- to 5-foot sleeping angel sharks. These placid bottom dwellers permit divers to observe them up close, sometimes even allowing them to pet their backs.

The rocky reef portions of Ship Rock feature a series of ledges and crevices that provide a habitat for scallops and lobsters. Colorful pink gorgonian fans are found throughout the wall sections. To be sure, Ship Rock is one of Catalina's best, but due to the depth involved, diving here is best left for the experienced.

33. BIRD ROCK: SEAWARD WALL

DEPTH:	25-120 FEET
LEVEL:	NOVICE TO EXPERIENCED

Bird Rock is one of Catalina Island's most frequented dive sites, yet not everyone visiting this area is familiar with its seaward wall.

The waters on the isthmus side of the rock are generally shallow with a gradual slope to deeper water. The seaward wall at Bird Rock, however, drops dramatically. It dips at the water's edge to approximately 25 feet where a steep slope of jumbled boulders plunges to the sand bottom at 120 feet.

Kelp

While kelp is found off some of California's beaches, it does not compare to the thick and luxuriant beds surrounding the remote offshore islands. High mineral content, sewage outfall and bryzoan infestation have all contributed to the major reduction of coastal kelp beds. Fortunately, the offshore islands have not been affected although several years ago, the warm influx of the El Nino current from South America caused heavy damage.

Given the right conditions, California's most common type of kelp, *Macrocystis pyrifera*, can grow over one foot a day. Some kelp colonies reach the surface from a depth of 100 feet.

Kelp beds provide extraordinary habitats for all types of fishes especially juveniles which are not often found on exposed reefs or in open ocean. California's kelp beds offer divers a unique opportunity to explore as they soar through the lofty limbs of a sunlit and magical undersea hanging forest.

37. ARROW POINT

DEPTH:	50-100 FEET
LEVEL:	INTERMEDIATE TO EXPERIENCED

Arrow Point is a promontory on the mainland side of Catalina. Since it is open to adverse weather, the site is often blown out when afternoon westerly winds pick up. In calm conditions, however, Arrow Point's 50- to 100-foot depths host excellent diving. Although visibility is only moderate, the area is often a hearty producer of game. Its jumbled rock piles and scattered boulders yield lobster and abalone when in season. Spearfishing here can result in an enjoyable dinner as well.

38. EMERALD COVE (S)

DEPTH:	20-40 FEET
LEVEL:	NOVICE

Although mainly an anchorage, fun diving is in store at Emerald Cove for novice divers. The water is calm and visibility is usually good, though there is little in the way of spectacular terrain. Here, a shallow reef system, fringed with a smattering of kelp, marks a site that is often visited by charter boats doing checkout dives. Depth ranges to 40 feet maximum with visibility averaging 30 feet or more. Emerald Cove often provides an excellent protected dive site.

39. LION HEAD (S)

DEPTH:	5-40 FEET
LEVEL:	NOVICE

Located northwest of Cherry Cove, this small but accommodating anchorage close to shore offers enjoyable diving. Lion Head is a shallow reef ringed by a small kelp system offering protection from afternoon winds. It is often visited by dive boats for a last dive of the day

due to its shallow terrain and diversity of marine life. Rocky boulders slope down toward a sand bottom fringed with eel grass and bull kelp. It is difficult to attain depths of more than 40 feet here. Visibility runs in the 40- to 50-foot range. In the extreme shallows of 5 feet or less, an observant diver will find a cache of green abalone.

40. LOBSTER BAY

DEPTH:	30-70 FEET
LEVEL:	INTERMEDIATE TO EXPERIENCED

Lobster Bay is a typical low-visibility dive on the seaward side of Catalina. Completely exposed to open ocean swells and wind, conditions can be marginal at times. Visibility is generally not too good, often averaging in the 10- to 15-foot range. The surge in the shallow areas is guaranteed to keep a diver rolling back and forth with the heartbeat of the ocean. Typically, the terrain consists of a series of small boulders and rocks that give way to a gently sloping sand bottom at 30 feet. Venturing deeper, the sand drops off sharply. Here divers will encounter an occasional finger reef covered with gorgonian fans of every color imaginable.

While the site is not exceptionally picturesque, there are significant advantages to diving Lobster Bay. It can often be a game hunter's dream with large halibut in the sand, abalone in the extreme shallows, and of course, lobster when in season. Photographers are better off elsewhere.

41. CAT HEAD

DEPTH:	15-130+ FEET
LEVEL:	INTERMEDIATE TO EXPERIENCED

On the windward side of Catalina is a rocky promontory at the entrance to Catalina Harbor known as Cat Head. When the surf is running, waves crash high up the cliffs above the

Trips in search of blue sharks can be arranged out of Avalon. Special equipment and preparation are necessary to make the trip safe and successful.

waterline. This site can only be dived in optimum conditions.

A stone's throw from the washrocks, the depth drops sharply to over 200 feet. Care must be taken to avoid going too deep, but there is plenty of depth to escape the surge. Visibility is usually low, often averaging 20 to 30 feet.

Cat Head is home to a variety of interesting rock and boulder formations, and finger reefs that descend into deeper water. Scores of colorful sea fans and anemones thrive along the ledges. For an extra bonus, visit the scattered and decaying remains of two long forgotten shipwrecks whose debris lies scattered in 50- to 70-foot range.

42. BLUE CAVERN POINT

DEPTH:	35-100+ FEET
LEVEL:	INTERMEDIATE TO EXPERIENCED

This rocky point, jutting from the eastern end of Isthmus Cove, is known for its vertical walls that plummet from the waterline to the bottom 90 to 100 feet deep. The rapidly sloping sand continues into deeper depths. Proper attention to dive planning and buoyancy control is a must to avoid descending too deep. Because of the depth and the currents that often sweep the site, Blue Cavern is for experienced divers only.

Gorgonian fans of all colors thrive, making the rock wall dance with a vibrant spectrum of life. Kelp encircles certain portions of the site offering a lush undersea garden. Visibility can be equal to the best found on the island.

43. SHARK CAGE DIVING

DEPTH:	10-30+ FEET
LEVEL:	INTERMEDIATE TO EXPERIENCED

Veteran diver and instructor Steve Whitaker organizes trips out of Avalon for bluewater cage dives in search of blue sharks. These trips are tremendously popular and his success rate in bringing in sharks is high.

The dive boat runs several miles off the coast where the shark cage is lowered over the side. After laying out a chum line of squid and mackerel, the blue sharks arrive and the divers head for the cage. On some trips, as many as 30 to 40 sharks buzz the cage at one time causing a quick release of adrenaline among the divers. Strobes begin firing like a barrage of magnesium flares. While a great opportunity to obtain high voltage action shots, photographers need to keep a calm eye and shutter finger.

These expeditions serve a research purpose as well. Often, Steve and his crew capture, weigh and tag the blue sharks for the California Department of Fish and Game.

CHAPTER **VIII**   FARNSWORTH BANK

Refer to map on page 21.

Farnsworth Bank, one of the Pacific's grandest open ocean seamounts, is less than a three hour boat ride from Los Angeles. Here, divers descend through the expanse of blue water to the waiting thermocline shimmering below in the depths. Silver and blue blacksmith part before the divers as the wall below slowly materializes.

At 110 feet, the water is clear enough to see the dive boat on the surface. Regulator exhaust bubbles resonate with a familiar metallic ring, and divers carefully monitor their depth and air supply. When they finally level off, divers are suspended over the cobalt blue water of the distance and depths. The colorful hydrocorals branch off the wall in a dazzling array of vermillion and lavender. Tranquility prevails.

HISTORY

Recreational anglers have long known that Farnsworth's deep water summit attracts rock fish, bass and other marine delicacies. When divers began visiting the site during the 50's and 60's, Farnsworth's fame as a seafood resource spread further. They harvested large abalone, scallops and hydrocoral in abundance.

It soon became apparent that the resource was unable to handle the impact. Farnsworth Bank still retains resident populations of scallops, and at deeper depths, white abalone. Divers and fishermen are still permitted to take finned fish, elusive abalone and saucer-sized scallops. The colorful branches of purple coral, however, are now protected. The Federal Bureau of Land Management has designated Farnsworth Bank as a purple coral sanctuary. No purple coral may be harvested or damaged.

GEOGRAPHY

Two miles off Ben Weston Point on the backside of Catalina Island lies the Bank. It is composed of several pinnacles some of which rise off the sand bottom from hundreds of feet to within 60 feet of the surface. The plateaus of these undersea peaks are small and offer little room for a boatload of divers to congregate. In addition, even if the dive boat is fortunate enough to anchor in shallow water, it is very easy for the anchor to drag into deeper water.

DIVING

Because it is hard to get the boat anchored on the shallow plateau, divers should plan on a dive to the 100-foot plus range. Divers will also discover a greater abundance of marine life in the 90- to 110-foot range.

Though diving at Farnsworth Bank requires many considerations and offers little margin for error, it is by no means dangerous. Hundreds of experienced divers safely visit Farnsworth every year without incident.

The only drawback to diving Farnsworth Bank is the limited amount of bottom time available because of the depths. Cruising along Farnsworth's flowering walls of yellow anemones, it is tantalizingly easy to become caught up with the rhapsody of the deep water scene and overstay a safe welcome. Dive time always seems to slip away unnoticed. With adequate planning, preparation and good common sense, divers will experience diving that is both exciting and rewarding.

The purple hydrocorals commonly seen in deeper water at Farnsworth Bank are protected from harvesting.

The brightly colored garibaldi, a highly territorial damselfish, is common in the southern group of islands.

Although bottom time at Farnsworth Bank is limited due to its depth, a carefully planned dive can be both rewarding and safe. A planned safety stop is always a good idea.

44. PURPLE HYDROCORAL

DEPTH:	60-130+ FEET
LEVEL:	EXPERIENCED

The dive sites at Farnsworth Bank are a series of Loran numbers.

An abundance of California hydrocoral thriving on Farnsworth's deeper walls makes these sites unique. Close cousins to tropical staghorn coral, these branching corals can vary in color from light lavender to bright red and pink. California hydrocorals are usually found on offshore pinnacles and reefs where stronger, open ocean currents generally prevail. These filter feeders extend tiny polyps from their calcareous skeletons to catch the plankton floating in the current. Hydrocorals are extremely slow growing. At Farnsworth, divers begin to encounter small concentrations of these hydrocorals near 90 feet, but they are more abundant at depths ranging from 100 to 210 feet.

Farnsworth Bank is also well known for its varietal anemone population. Large anemones are particularly prolific. Clustered onto the rocks and ledges among the corals, divers will find an array of bright red, pink, white and lavender corynactus anemones. Moonglow, proliferating and tealia anemones can be found clutching the rocky headlands exposed to open current. While the large anemones tend to live a semi-solitary existence, the sociable yellow anemone can be found in groups transforming huge vertical ledges into vibrant and living masterpieces. These yellow anemones reproduce sexually as well as by budding—an occurrence during which an anemone literally "pulls itself in half," forming two complete animals. Divers unfamiliar with these small but iridescent anemones are often taken aback to discover a yellow field of anemones the size of a billboard.

Nestled within the colonial anemone fields lie mottled varieties of scorpionfish. The hues of the anemones vary greatly, and scorpionfish find a patch suitable for their personal camouflage to blend into the scenery.

Farnsworth's open ocean position leaves it exposed to prevailing currents and swell, producing water clarity that is excellent. Cold ocean currents funnel deep water nutrients to the area's filter-feeding organisms while providing some of the best visibility available near Catalina Island. With the current also comes occasional yellowtail, barracuda, white sea bass and silvery schools of baitfish. An ever present population of blacksmith hovers within the thermocline.

Caution. Farnsworth is a deep dive, with the prospect of becoming an extremely deep dive for those unable to control buoyancy and monitor depth properly. Air consumption increases fourfold or more during an average dive at Farnsworth, making monitoring of pressure gauges critical. Bouyancy must be carefully maintained to avoid an uncontrolled descent to depths deeper than planned.

Before entering the water at Farnsworth Bank, divers should carefully consider their depth, time and air supply limitations. Divers should not release their grip from the anchor line until directly on the reef. When the boat is bucking viciously, use the line as a reference. Be aware, however, that releasing the line a few feet before reaching the pinnacle can spell trouble when a current is running. The unwary diver may easily be blown off the seamount and carried away in the current. On reaching the bottom, divers should orient themselves to their surroundings and the anchor line. The ability to return to the anchor line is essential for a safe and controlled ascent and allows divers to make a saftey stop at ten to fifteen feet.

A ring spotted dorid grazes on the reef. Dorids are a suborder of the nudibranch family.

CHAPTER IX SANTA BARBARA ISLAND

Refer to map on page 23.

Santa Barbara Island, despite its diminutive size, offers a wealth of underwater opportunity. The availability of sites here at the smallest of the Channel Islands offers an abundance of aquatic adventure and is truly representative of some of California's best diving.

HISTORY

This small island has little of the cultural and historical color of the other outposts in the Channel Islands. Lacking in natural resources such as firewood and water, Santa Barbara Island did not host an Indian population. Archeological evidence indicates that Santa Barbara Island was used as a stopover campsite for Indian hunting parties searching for sea lions and sea otters. Fish hook fragments found in old middens indicate that the island may have been used for tribal fishing expeditions as well. To the Channel Islands Indians, Santa Barbara Island was merely a layover for canoeing parties trading between the northern and southern islands.

The island has no adequate anchorages for large sailing vessels, so most early sea captains found refuge from inclement weather at the larger islands to the north and south, or took their chances in the open sea. Most shore expeditions were confined to landing on the northeast end of the island, directly below the mesa near Arch Point.

The early Spanish explorers did not give the small land mass much thought. Very little was written about it in ships' logbooks. One explorer, however, did take the time and effort to bestow a name to the small land mass. On December 4, 1602, Spanish explorer Sebastian Vizcaino named the island "Saint Barbara." After his passage, the island was not to be visited by another exploratory party for 100 years.

Eventually, control of Alta California and its offshore islands passed from Spain to Mexico. At the conclusion of the war between the United States and Mexico, Santa Barbara Island became United States territory. Unlike many of its neighbors, the island was never privately owned. During this period, there was minimal American activity at the island, save for brief visits by smugglers, sea lion and otter hunters, and fishermen. Several leases were granted to private individuals for ranching and farming purposes. At the turn of the century, the Hyder family engaged in raising sheep, and growing barley, hay and potatoes on the island. They enjoyed only limited success and abandoned the island in 1922. Interestingly, the Hyders relocated to San Pedro and opened a sportfishing business called 22nd Street Landing. Still in operation today, many of their boats bring visiting divers to the Hyders' former homestead.

In 1938, Santa Barbara Island became part of the Channel Islands National Monument, and is currently managed by the Department of the Interior and the National Park Service. The Park Service maintains the landing facility and a visitor's station on the southwest side of the island. A small Quonset hut serves as lodging for Park Service Rangers and there are five primitive camping sites near the Station. Permission to camp may be obtained through the Channel Islands Visitor's Center in Ventura. Numerous land-based visitors come to Santa Barbara Island to photograph its large population of rare birds.

GEOGRAPHY

If dynamite comes in small packages, then Santa Barbara Island possesses an explosive

A Spanish shawl nudibranch crawls across a diver's gloved finger.

alone. Be sure the aperture is readjusted to accommodate the faster shutter speed.

49. RUBSCHLAGER REEF

DEPTH:	35-50 FEET
LEVEL:	INTERMEDIATE

Named after the intrepid lobster hunter Jens Rubschlager, this site is located on the windward side of the island between Sutil Island and Webster Point. Because of the barren terrain, photographers won't find much interest here. The bottom is mostly covered by flat rocks with numerous purple sea urchins and gorgonian fans. There is no kelp in this area.

At first glance, it appears to be a wasteland in the middle of nowhere. Of special interest to lobster hunters, however, are the piles of rocks that resemble coral heads. These mounds have shallow crevices that are usually packed with lobster—sometimes as many as forty. Unfortunately, the site has been heavily impacted so most of the crustaceans are undersized. Usually there will be a legal specimen for every six "shorts." Be sure to measure your catch before putting it in your game bag.

50. SUTIL ISLAND

DEPTH:	20-130+ FEET
LEVEL:	INTERMEDIATE TO
	EXPERIENCED

This is a small islet located at the southwest end of Santa Barbara Island. Its towering land mass looms above the dense kelp bed and several wash rocks close to shore. The perimeter ranges in depths from 20 to over 130 feet and features numerous walls, canyons and caves.

Protective cows may feel their offspring are being threatened and even fun-loving sea lions have been known to bite. Also at certain times of year, the bulls take offense when divers venture too close to their female "harems." Since these aggressive males can reach proportions of several hundred pounds, it is best to give them a wide berth.

The Rookery is slightly more barren than other sites at Santa Barbara Island, but the sea lions with their playful antics more than make up for it. Indeed, sightseeing divers and photographers are now begging boat captains to visit the rookery much to the chagrin of game taking enthusiasts. Once in the water, however, even the most dedicated hunter will chuckle watching sea lions run through their paces.

Photo Tip. Divers wishing to photograph sea lions should do so with a wide-angle lens and an extremely fast shutter speed. At least 250th to 500th of a second is needed to compensate for the bursts of speed that the sea lions are capable of achieving. Nikonos cameras with strobes do not synchronize this fast, so the photographer must rely on available light

Colorful invertebrates and fish abound off Sutil Island at the southwest end of Santa Barbara Island.

Lobsters can often be found off Santa Barbara Island and make a tasty after-dive dinner.

A favorite lobster spot for commercial fishermen, divers will encounter rusting and destroyed traps throughout the area. The wind usually picks up in the afternoon, but dive boats can almost always find a calm anchorage.

Photographers will delight in the abundance of fish and colorful invertebrates. Reef residents range from a plethora of brittle stars and colorful gorgonian fans to dozens of varieties of nudibranchs. Spearfishermen find Sutil Island attractive due to the large sheepshead and occasional yellowtail that pass through the area. Depending on conditions, Sutil can also produce large lobster.

Visibility at Sutil Island is usually good, averaging from 30 to 70 feet or more depending on conditions.

Caution. Divers should exercise caution when venturing near the cave. Surges can unexpectedly pull divers dangerously deep inside these catacombs. The caves should be accessed only by experienced cave divers on the calmest of days. Some caves run through the entire islet.

51. SHAG ROCK

DEPTH:	30-50 FEET
LEVEL:	INTERMEDIATE

Shag Rock is a smaller eroded islet located between Webster Point and Arch Point on the northwest side of Santa Barbara Island. Lying closer to Santa Barbara Island than Sutil Island, it is also densely forested with a thick kelp bed. Depths are shallower here, making it difficult for divers to go beyond 50 feet.

The terrain is composed of a rocky reef interspersed with patches of sand, making it a good site for halibut and abalone hunting. Portions of the reef drop to the sand at about 30 feet and form small wall structures with overhanging ledges. Be sure to inspect these during lobster season.

Unfortunately, visibility at Shag Rock is not great, usually running in the 15- to 20-foot range. In the fall and winter months when storms are not present, visibility is greater.

Angel sharks. As divers venture into the shallows at Shag Rock, the terrain becomes more picturesque and the increased ambient light improves visibility. Although surge is often present in shallow depths, divers may encounter large (and docile) sleeping angel sharks on the sand patches near the reefs. These sleeping creatures will often permit the gentle diver to pet them underwater. It is always a thrill to return home and tell your dive buddies that you spent the day petting 5-foot sharks. The sleeping sharks make a great photo opportunity.

52. AB CITY (S)

DEPTH:	5-25 FEET
LEVEL:	NOVICE TO
	INTERMEDIATE

Located just inshore and west of Shag Rock is the famous area known as Ab City. A small sea lion and elephant seal rookery lies approximately 100 yards from the site that is also marked by a large landslide that fell from the towering cliffs above.

Abalone galore. Why would anyone want to subject themselves to heavy surge and 5 to 10 feet of visibilty for a "fun" dive? The answer is culinary delight. In 25 feet of water, it is possible for divers to bring back a legal day's limit of abalone in short order. It is almost impossible not to be successful here unless a diver loses his abalone iron. There are few photo opportunities at this game site.

Many boat operators voluntarily limit the number of divers they place in the area to help preserve the resource, which is still relatively abundant after many years.

MARINE MAMMALS

Divers visiting offshore California are bound to be treated to a visit by any combination of resident marine mammals. Harbor seals and California sea lions are most common. These playful creatures will often follow divers underwater, nibbling on fins and staring at their reflection in camera lenses. Other species found in northern island groups (like San Miguel) are Stellar sea lions, guadalupe fur seals, and the largest of all—the raggle-snouted elephant seal which can weigh over 1,000 pounds.

Mammals usually encountered during boat trips to various dive sites are varieties of dolphins, porpoises and whales. Gray whales migrate along the California coast annually.

Occasionally, finback or breeching humpback whales are seen.

Measure abalone underwater. Remember to measure your abalone with a California Department of Fish and Game approved caliper before removing the abalone. Often, abalone removed from the rocks may be cut in the process and will not survive. Once you feel that the abalone is legal, double check it underwater. There are stiff fines for bringing undersized abalone on the boat. Fish and Game officials are vigilant and often board dive boats unexpectedly.

53. WEBSTER POINT CAVES

DEPTH:	40-90+ FEET
LEVEL:	INTERMEDIATE TO EXPERIENCED

On the windward side of Santa Barbara Island, just slightly southeast of Webster Point, lies a spectacular area with good visibility, kelp, diverse terrain, and several small caves and caverns. These formations offer divers the opportunity to swim through archways and overhangs with chimney chutes, while maintaining visual contact with daylight most of the time.

This reef area is barren, flat and rocky. It gives way to ledges with surge channels and vertical walls. Fine granulated sand and cobblestone pebbles are often found at the base of these formations. Sea urchins, gorgonians and brittle stars are plentiful here, as are thick-horned aeolids *(Hermissenda crassicornis)*, a colorful type of nudibranch.

Dragon Cave. The main feature is called Dragon Cave by several charter boat operators. To get here, divers drop off a wall at 90 feet and discover a large overhang that recedes far back into the reef. It is a long, serpentine cavern with a large opening that narrows far back inside.

Lights are an added advantage as it gets quite dark in the inner recesses. Approximately 40 feet inside the crevice, a chimney chute opens, sending shafts of daylight cascading through the rear and allowing divers to exit onto a shallow section of the reef. Water inside the crevice is calm and still, and lobster can occasionally be found there. The Dragon Cave

The kelp beds off Santa Barbara Island are majestic and awe inspiring, especially when sunlight filters down through the fronds.

near Webster Point is always thrilling for those who venture though it. Photographers are presented with excellent opportunities here as well.

Due to an almost constant surge, it is usually most comfortable to stay below 50 feet. But, on a calm sunny day the entire region southeast of Webster Point offers spectacular diving with visibility reaching the 80-foot mark. On these special days there is nothing quite like swimming through the sun-dappled channels, walls and caverns at Webster Point. It is often so good that a boat captain may decide to stay for several dives so divers can experience the wide variety of terrain.

Large sheepshead, ocean whitefish and calico bass frequent this area, and sightseers stand a good chance of encountering bat rays or Pacific electric rays here as well.

CHAPTER X OIL DRILLING PLATFORMS

Refer to map on page 21.

Offshore oil drilling platforms are a volatile subject in California. Although the oil rigs themselves had nothing to do with the February 1990 crude oil spill at Huntington Beach (when a British petroleum tanker punctured its hold), the tide of public opinion against oil companies and their operations has been turning decidedly negative.

Environmentalists consider the rigs a blight on the horizon. As the oil companies continue to receive unfavorable press, the controversy surrounding the offshore oil rigs gains momentum. At the heart of the issue is not only whether new rigs should be prohibited, but whether present ones should continue to exist.

In the midst of current controversy, the rigs have found an advocate as an increasing number of recreational divers seek access to dive these artificial reef structures.

The rigs are a significant attraction for marine life. Schools of fish teem throughout the iron columns and scores of invertebrates thrive on the structures themselves.

Unfortunately, in the Golden State, access to oil rigs is usually restricted without written permission. Due to the environmental controversy of the rigs and the legal climate in California, the oil companies view visiting divers as more of a threat than benefit.

HISTORY

Oil is nothing new to California. Deposits have been so rich that early Chumash Indians made their canoes watertight with the natural seepage that washed ashore. Today, natural seepage still occurs as oil deposits break from the sea floor and drift ashore in small amounts. If you are walking on the beach and accidentally get tar on your feet, chances are that this was just another normal geological seepage.

Oil drilling in California has been a profitable venture since the 1920's. The 1950's saw drilling wells move from the beach to offshore locations, and since then a profusion of platforms have been erected from Huntington Beach to Point Conception. Some rigs have as many as 20 wells running off them.

In the early 1970's, a major blowout occurred off Santa Barbara, dumping massive amounts of heavy crude oil onto local beaches. Since then, many coastal residents view the rigs as unsightly and worry that another damaging spill could occur.

Their fears were increased when the oil tanker, *American Trader* dumped over 300,000 gallons of light Alaskan crude oil on the sand between Seal and Laguna Beach, killing many birds and fouling the shoreline.

GEOGRAPHY

The rigs are man-made iron islands positioned in deepwater plains of barren sand. In a way, the rigs are similar to open ocean pinnacles, which serve as attraction for marine life. There is a significant marine ecosystem flourishing beneath the water's surface on these oil rigs.

Once the rigs are erected, marine encrustation begins immediately. Before long, myriads of sea creatures congregate on and around the rigs. Only a small, but growing handful of divers and biologists is aware of how important these structures have become for the marine ecology.

California's offshore oil rigs are a veritable Garden of Eden in the middle of a wilderness.

While offshore oil rigs are of some environmental concern, their structures have created habitats which are now diverse ecosystems thriving with marine life.

When two obsolete rigs were torn down near Point Conception, a thriving marine environment was decimated in the process. The ultimate irony is that these structures were hauled on a barge to Los Angeles Harbor, hydrowashed and prepared for redepositing in Santa Monica Bay as artificial reef structures. "Heal The Bay," an environmental group objected to the dumping of the rigs for fish habitat purpose. The plan was scrapped; a resource was destroyed for nothing.

DIVING

Recently, the oil companies have begun to allow divers access to some rigs on a permit

Diving through the support stanchions of oil rigs is a surreal experience accompanied by awesome visibility and a plethora of marine life.

basis that requires signing a liability waiver. Probably the best rig diving is in the Santa Barbara Channel. Closer to shore are rigs with names such as Heidi, Hogan, Houchin, Hazel, Hilda and Henry. Farther from shore is Hill House and Platforms A, B and C. Farthest from shore still near Point Conception is the lonely and wave-battered Hondo rig.

54. THE RIGS

DEPTH:	40-130+ FEET
LEVEL:	EXPERIENCED

While the shallower rigs closer to shore are prone to surge and dirty water, the outer rigs are enthralling. Visibility can exceed 100 feet or more. Massive schools of juvenile fish dart throughout the iron structures, while mature bass lurk off in the distance. Bait fish sweep through the columns like explosive silver phantoms, creating scenery reminiscent of more tropical Pacific climates. The iron supports offer a bedazzling tapestry of invertebrate life. Colorful anemones, and sponges of every size and color are stratified in zones of lavender, green, blue, red and white. Giant white-plumed Metridium anemones stretch into the current, transforming the massive columns into a snow-like field of filter feeders. Huge mussels grow in the intertidal shallows, washed almost constantly by rich currents that flow through the rig. Giant sea stars, ochre stars, and colorful rainbow stars feed among the platforms' lush coverage of exceptionally large scallops and oysters. The only familiar California sea dweller absent on the rigs is kelp.

   Diving the oil rigs is like flying through an unfinished skyscraper. All about are girders and columns resembling a giant undersea erector set. Yet, not only does a diver get to soar through the massive support systems, he has the opportunity to encounter an incredible amount of marine life. The deep water oil rigs off the southern California coast rival any natural pinnacle mentioned in this book. Nowhere else is marine life so profuse and colorful, and for every 20 feet or so the diver descends, a new neighborhood of creatures is encountered.

On a calm day, the best place to explore is the 15- to 20-foot shallows. Here, huge starfish wrap their legs around the struts as large barnacles extend their sweeping filter strainers into the current. Thousands of juvenile fish teem through the rig's interior. On sun-washed days, visibility is staggering, and the water comfortably warm.

Dropping down to the 40-foot range, walls of red, blue and pink corynactus blanket the structures. Venturing deeper still to 60 feet and more, the Metridium population takes over. The large, white feather duster anemones plummet in large rows into the gloomy abyss below.

Caution. Care must be taken when diving the offshore rigs. As with any other wall-type dive, it is easy to go deeper and stay longer than planned. It is important therefore to monitor depth, time and air supply. If there is ever a place in southern California where divers will be tempted to go deeper than planned, the oil rigs are it. The incredible displays of marine life along the vertical pillars are a siren's call that must be ignored. Most of the rigs bottom out in dimly lit sand depths at 200 feet. Some rigs farther north and out to sea, such as Hondo are even much deeper.

Large Metridium anemones proliferate on the rigs, creating frilly carpets of white.

Multi-colored starfish and a variety of invertebrates cover the rig's structural supports.

CHAPTER **XI** ANACAPA ISLAND

Refer to map on page 25.

The Anacapa Island group is the southernmost of the northern group of the Santa Barbara Channel Islands.

Anacapa lies a short distance offshore from Port Hueneme and fast private boats can make the crossing in less than half an hour. Charter dive boats take approximately an hour and a half. Its proximity to shore offers divers a tremendous resource close to home.

Anacapa Island, whose name was derived from the Chumash Indian word *eneepah* that means "ever changing" or "deception," has often preplexed navigators. Sailing straight southeast for Anacapa from neighboring Santa Cruz, the three table-top like islets appear to be one land mass. Heading south out of Ventura Harbor, all three islands are easily discernable. On a clear mainland day, residents of Santa Monica and Malibu may only discern two of the islands.

The Anacapa Islands are often considered Ventura County's version of Catalina Island since it is one of the most heavily visited by divers. Yet despite the abundance of boat traffic and visitors from the mainland in the summer, Anacapa is well worth the visit.

HISTORY

This group of islands was first discovered by Juan Rodriguez Cabrillo in 1542.

Except for occasional visits from hunters and pirates, the three small, flat islets of the Anacapa group received little attention until 1853 when the Pacific Mail steamship *Winfield Scott* slammed onto the rocky shore of one of the islands. A navigational light was not installed until 1911 when government funds were appropriated. In the meantime, several other ships came to grief on Anacapa's shores.

Prior to the turn of the century, the Anacapa Islands were frequented by fishermen, whalers and seal hunters. One such visitor was early California explorer George Nidever who hunted seal and sea otter in the kelp beds.

The Treaty of Guadalupe Hidalgo at the conclusion of the war between the United States and Mexico, gave California and its offshore islands to the United States. Anacapa Island was leased to several entrepreneurs who established sheep ranching and fishing concessions. Anacapa, as was the case with other Channel Islands, became a smuggler's haven during prohibition years.

Today, a different breed of adventurer comes to the shores of the Channel Islands.

The northern islands of Anacapa, Santa Cruz, Santa Rosa and San Miguel are a marine sanctuary. Since Anacapa is part of the Channel Islands National Park and regulated by the Park Service, it receives hundreds of above-water visitors annually. The island is accessible on a limited basis to visiting naturalists for hiking and overnight camping.

GEOGRAPHY

The three islets comprising Anacapa are named East, Middle and West Islands. Anacapa is the second smallest of all the northern and southern Channel Islands.

Anacapa's most striking physical attraction is the famous archway located at the extreme end of East Anacapa Island. This marine arch was created by thousands of years of erosion and wave action. The islands can be seen from a long distance, for farther above the waterline, the geological profile is extreme with some peaks cresting at over 900 feet. Its shores are relatively steep, barricaded by cliffs on all

Anacapa's Cathedral Cove is a protected ecological reserve abundant with marine life and photo opportunities.

*Although Anacapa appears to be one
land mass when approached from
certain directions, the island group is
actually comprised of three islets.
Photo: Courtesy of the National Park
Service.*

sides. The island is composed of weathered
volcanic Miocene rock. What Anacapa lacks
in above water size, it makes up with
underwater variety and abundance.

DIVING

Numerous underwater fissures, caves and
caverns ring the islets. Ledges, rocky reefs,
walls, drop-offs and opulent kelp beds have
beckoned many divers over the years. Sea
lions, cup corals, gorgonians, nudibranchs,
anemones, moon snails, bat rays, horn sharks,
lobster, abalone and a variety of starfish are all
part of the thriving aquatic life that makes up
the natural aquarium at Anacapa.

Anacapa generally hosts phenomenal
underwater visibility especially in the calm
spring and summer months when it can reach
more than 100 feet. When abundant plankton
is in the water, visibility can be reduced
severely.

Some areas of the islands are closed to
fishing and underwater game collecting. On
the mainland side of East Anacapa, no aquatic
specimens may be taken in less than 60 feet of
water. Also on the mainland side from the
junction of East Anacapa and Middle Anacapa
to Keyhole Rock, divers may spear seasonal
fish, but not take invertebrate life such as
scallops, lobster or abalone. The same rules
apply on the seaward side of West Anacapa
Island between Frenchy's Cove and Cat Rock.

To add to the confusion, no vessels may
come within a third of a mile offshore between
Frenchy's Cove and the middle seaward side of
West Anacapa from January to October as it is
a California brown pelican nesting area.

EAST ANACAPA ISLAND

55. ARCH ROCK

DEPTH:	55-80+ FEET
LEVEL:	EXPERIENCED

Arch Rock is located a short distance from the
Anacapa lighthouse. Strong currents usually
sweep through the area and the rocks are
densely covered with kelp. The terrain is steep,
dropping quickly from the shallows to 80 feet.
This area is also part of Anacapa's ecological

WHISTLER'S SEAGULLS

Like the famous sea-arch at Cabo San Lucas and other prominent spots along the Pacific Coast, Arch Rock was creatively sculpted by wave action and erosion over hundreds of years. In 1854 this 40-foot tall archway was drawn by artist James Whistler whose engraved sketches were made during a United States expedition to survey the West Coast. Whistler incorporated "artistic license" in his drawing of the arch by adding a flock of seagulls to his engraving. After a warning from his supervisor to cease with such artistic touches, Whistler left the gulls in the engraving anyway. Unfortunately it cost him his job and a subsequent rework of the engraving by another artist deleted the gulls.

reserve, so the "take pictures, leave bubbles, keep memories" rule is in effect. While game seekers avoid this end of the island, photographers will be well rewarded.

The reefs running off Arch Rock are continually fed by prevailing currents, making it an excellent site for photographing anemones and gorgonians. As with most of the offshore islands and pinnacles, visibility is best during late summer and early fall months. When conditions are favorable, the Arch Rock

Anacapa offers a large variety of dive experiences — enough to make every diver happy.

area can feature visibility exceeding 100 feet— a tremendous treat for any offshore diver!

56. CATHEDRAL COVE

DEPTH:	20-40 FEET
LEVEL:	NOVICE

An ecological reserve in the center of East Anacapa Island, Cathedral Cove faces the mainland. When the northwesterly winds are calm, Cathedral Cove is a placid anchorage with rock-lined shores. Several outcroppings

jut from the shore and are used by sea lions and harbor seals as a haul out. Thick kelp spreads over the entire area and marine life thrives. Because of the area's protected status, Cathedral Cove was not often visited. Since the increased popularity of underwater photography and videography, this site is receiving more visitors who want to look, explore and enjoy without affecting the environment.

If divers would like a good look at the Anacapa Island of ten years ago, protected areas like Cathedral Cove are the place to do it. Large sheepshead thrive here, as do big calico bass, abalone, scallops and schools of teeming reef fish.

The terrain at Cathedral Cove is unique. Its small series of wash rocks give way to miniature underwater walls, canyons and ledges. Depths generally do not exceed 40 feet, unless one swims farther offshore beyond the kelp. Visibility averages 30 feet.

Caution. Visitors should be advised to stay clear of the area when strong northwest winds and swell are present. These conditions create a hazardous anchorage at Cathedral Cove.

MIDDLE ANACAPA ISLAND

57. EAST FISH CAMP

DEPTH:	25-55 FEET
LEVEL:	NOVICE

Located on the seaward side of Middle Anacapa Island, East Fish Camp is an anchorage that provides protection from northwesterly wind and swell. When an unusual south swell picks up, however, the opposite side of the island offers the best anchorage.

East Fish Camp features several low-lying, rocky reefs with a gently sloping drop-off composed of sand and cobblestones. As an anchorage, the area is attractive, but game is scarce. Except for a few sea urchins, sea cucumbers, starfish and anemones the reefs are relatively sparse. The sand patches between kelp beds are often home to squadrons of large bat rays.

Hunters and photographers, however, should not discount East Fish Camp, for remember the rule of anchorages: when there is believed to be no game left, a persistent diver will suprise everyone by coming back to the boat with a 50-pound halibut, 10-pound lobster, or a monster abalone.

WEST ANACAPA ISLAND

58. CORAL REEF

DEPTH:	20-90 FEET
LEVEL:	INTERMEDIATE

The northwestern corner of West Anacapa tends to receive the majority of diver traffic from nearby Ventura Harbor. Immediately seaward on the West End's last rocky point lies a lush kelp bed with extremely clear water known as Coral Reef. Heavy currents can, at times, rip through the area, causing the kelp to lay flat along the bottom. But when the currents die down, water clarity usually remains and great diving awaits.

The name Coral Reef was bestowed on this site because of the numerous stone corals that dot the rocks and ledges in deeper water. The terrain within the kelp bed is a mass of jumbled rock piles and ledges at a depth range of 20 to 40 feet.

Harbor seals. Be forewarned that this kelp bed is a harbor seal hangout. These fat, stubby, cigar-shaped relatives of the California sea lion are extremely curious critters and will bring the whole gang along to check out the strange looking creatures with the bubble-blowing machines on their backs. Don't be alarmed if they nibble on your fins, sniff at your goody bag and chase your bubbles. Harbor seals are friendly for the most part, but they will try to talk you out of a fish or two if you have one hanging on a stringer.

At approximately 45 feet, the kelp thins out and a vertical wall drops downward to a sand bottom. At 80 to 90 feet, small rock piles sit alone in the sand, home to colorful gorgonians, stone corals and a wide variety of invertebrates. Occasionally, a legal-sized lobster or two may be hiding beneath the ledges.

59. CAT ROCK

DEPTH:	20-60 FEET
LEVEL:	NOVICE

Farther down the line on West Anacapa is a foul area known as Cat Rock consisting of several tall pinnacles known as Cat Rock that jut above the surging waterline. A popular diving area, Cat Rock's promontories and the nearby island cliffs often provide a calm anchorage for boats. The terrain is shallow, and only after swimming a considerable distance do the ledges slope into the 60-foot range.

Currents are relatively mild and the surface is usually calm. Since divers can stay as shallow as they care to, Cat Rock is usually chosen as a "last dive of the day" spot. As with most of Anacapa, there is a thick kelp bed in the vicinity. The bottom in the shallows tends to look a little barren, but closer observation will yield a host of invertebrate life. A variety of nudibranchs inhabit the area and are excellent subjects for the macro photographer's extension tubes. When the diving day draws to a close, Cat Rock is a splendid place to peel off the wet suit and soak up some sun before turning into the prevailing northwesterly afternoon winds and heading home.

60. WEST ANACAPA CLIFFS

DEPTH:	40-75 FEET
LEVEL:	NOVICE TO
	INTERMEDIATE

Around the corner from Coral Reef and approximately half-way down West Anacapa is where the island reaches its highest point in elevation at 930 feet. Anchoring due west of Summit Peak is a dive site featuring sheer rock walls draped by a thick kelp bed dropping into 45 feet of water.

This is the last accessible point on the front of West Anacapa Island before entering the restricted zone for nesting pelicans. The nesting zone is open to divers and boat traffic from January 1 to October 31. With one exception (Frenchy's Cove), no landings are permitted anywhere on West Anacapa at any time of the year.

The small finger reefs are interspersed with sand and provide excellent habitats for resting angel sharks and occasional halibut. Beyond the edges of the kelp beds, the terrain quickly slopes off to 95 feet. Here, unwary divers can quickly find themselves deeper than they expected. Visibility usually averages 20 to 30 feet, but can improve greatly in late summer and early fall.

Nudibranchs. At various seasons throughout the year, photographers will delight in the rainbow of nudibranchs in this area. Usually encountered are bright purple and vermillion Spanish shawls (*Flabellinopsis iodinea*), as well as light blue, white and yellow thick-horned aeolids (*Hermissendas crassicornis*). The nudibranchs abound in a variety of sizes, presenting opportunities for extension tubes of every kind.

61. FRENCHY'S COVE (S)

DEPTH:	10-35 FEET
LEVEL:	NOVICE

This is the only spot on West Anacapa where landings are permitted. Frenchy's is the last portion of West Anacapa Island before a series of wash rocks stretches to Middle Anacapa. The relief drops lower in this area, and the cliffs of West Anacapa form a protective bight where boaters can escape the incoming wind and swell. Frenchy's features one of Anacapa's only sandy beaches, with coarse granular sand and cobblestones flanked by rocks and tide pools.

Excellent snorkeling. This is an excellent snorkeling spot and is often visited by passing sailboats that spend their summers cruising the entire chain. Frenchy's is not a protected area. Divers can hunt and fish here, although no species may be taken from the tide pools.

Kelp is sparse in this area, with visiblity averaging 20 to 30 feet. A shallow spot, divers will be hard pressed to find areas deeper than 35 feet.

62. FOOTPRINT REEF SHARK DIVING

DEPTH:	5-30 FEET
LEVEL:	EXPERIENCED

By and large, this is the highest voltage attraction at Anacapa Island. Located over three miles offshore in the gap between Anacapa and Santa Cruz Islands, Footprint Reef rises to within 300 feet of the surface.

Although the bottom is 300 feet, the dives take place in the bluewater expanse above the Reef at depths usually no deeper than 30 feet. In fact, on a calm day, divers can idle their time away catching the fast-paced action of circling blue and mako sharks from the inside of a metal shark cage in only 8 feet of water.

Steve Maderas, owner of Scuba Luv Aquatics in Woodlands Hills and the dive boat, *Scuba Luv'r*, has been running weekly shark cage trips for several years. Steve and his crew have developed a highly productive method of attracting and keeping sharks in the area as the dive boat and cage drifts over Footprint Reef. Using a concoction of chopped frozen mackerel, squid and other marine goodies referred to as "Steve's Secret Sauce," crew members begin chumming the surface upon arrival at the reef site.

The boat heads into the current as the chum is dispersed, and then cuts engines, drifting backwards. The cage is lowered and the wait begins. When Steve's operation first began experimenting with different ways of attracting sharks, sometimes a lengthy wait would ensue. On rare occasions, sharks didn't show up at all. At the present, although there is no guarantee that sharks will be attracted, it appears that the "sauce" has been perfected. Sharks usually arrive within 20 to 30 minutes after ladling out the chum.

Visibility at Footprint Reef is usually excellent, often in excess of 70 feet. Of course, during periods when large amounts of plankton are present, visibility can be reduced to a mere 15 feet.

Usually one or two blue sharks will approach the chum line and floating bait boxes first, with several more arriving on their heels. Soon there may be half a dozen sharks, then a full dozen. On special days, dozens of sharks

The shark cage is positioned directly behind the boat's swim step.

swarm the waters around and beneath the cage. With so many blue sharks darting in and out of the area, it is easy to lose track of how many there are, but sightings of 30 sharks and more have not been uncommon.

Passengers are able to access the cage directly from the surface. The *Scuba Luv'r* cage is lifted into the water with a deck crane and floats by internal buoyancy tanks. Crew members swing the cage directly behind the swim step. Here, as the blue sharks mingle about the propellers and bait boxes, divers can simply roll face first inside the opening at the top of the cage.

Blue sharks are long and slender, ranging anywhere from 4 to over 11 feet in length. A pelagic shark, the blue is characterized by a striking iridescent blue upper body and a silvery-white lower body. This provides the shark with a degree of camouflage when viewed from the surface or when looking up from depth.

Divers can position themselves in the corners of the cage and point their camera lenses inches away from the passing sharks. Occasionally sharks glide nose first into cage bars, becoming stuck after wiggling partially inside the cage itself. Divers should bear in mind that the sharks really are not intent on coming inside the cage. In fact, they don't want anything to do with it. They are merely attracted by the bait in the water and the cage is just an inconvenience. On rare occasions, it is possible to have a small juvenile shark actually squirm its way through the metal lattice and wind up inside the cage itself! For those unfamilar with blue sharks, moments like this become very exciting. It is important to recognize that once the little shark realizes it is inside the cage, all it wants is out. A calm diver can simply push the youngster towards the opening at the top of the cage and it will swim out.

While the majority of sharks attracted on these trips are blues, occasionally makos burst onto the scene with lighting speed. Makos dwarf the blues and are formidable fish. Always be prepared to turn up your camera's shutter speed for the arrival of a mako. Their appearance is usually brief, but impressive.

Photo tip. When photographing sharks from a cage, remember that they will be moving at variable speeds and one should judge shutter speed and aperture calculations appropriately. As sharks roam the outside perimeter, focusing in and out with a housed SLR camera is not impossible, but it is difficult. A 15mm lens on an amphibious camera makes taking "the quick shot" much easier. Photographers using wide-angle lenses should not worry about getting close enough to their subjects, as it is often very simple to shoot within nine inches of a shark's nose.

Shark cage trips at Anacapa are always exciting. Rarely do more than six divers show up for a mid-week charter, giving divers plenty of time to shoot video tape or film of the action.

Steve Maderas' shark trips to Footprint Reef often attract several dozen or more sharks at the same time.

Sharks come right up to the cage, giving photographers some great adrenalin-filled photo opportunities.

CHAPTER XII SANTA CRUZ ISLAND

Refer to map on page 25.

Santa Cruz Island is the largest of all the Channel Islands, and it is especially endowed with an appropriate mix of anchorages and diving areas to meet every underwater explorer's needs. Regardless of what the weather is up to, one can always find many sites where conditions are good for diving.

The environment becomes distinctly different as one moves northward through the Channel Islands chain. Invertebrate life is more prolific, and divers begin encountering a greater variety of nudibranchs and anemones. Indeed, there are places where the marine life is so prolific that you cannot put your hand on a rock without coming in contact with another living creature.

HISTORY

Santa Cruz is an island as rich in history as natural resources. Following Cabrillo and Vizcaino's earlier explorations for Spain, Gaspar de Portola's supply vessels *San Carlos* and *San Antonio* explored Alta California's coast and offshore islands. Captain Juan Perez's ships visited several of the Channel Islands, including Santa Cruz in 1769. Historical sources credit Perez, who led Portola's expedition, with naming Santa Cruz Island. According to popular legend, as a party of Spaniards hiked along the island, one of the expedition's friars left behind a walking staff decorated with a small iron cross on its handle. The local Chumash Indians found the staff and returned it the following day. The explorers thus bestowed the island the name "Santa Cruz" meaning "Holy Cross."

Later, when the English adventurer George Vancouver extensively explored the Channel Islands in 1773, his resulting maps included an island named Santa Cruz. The name became permanent.

As with all of Alta California, control of the island later passed from Spain to Mexico and eventually to the United States. During this period, Santa Cruz Island felt the impact of western influence. The Franciscan friars had long considered building a mission similar to those already established on the mainland. In the mid-1700's, there were still hundreds of Indians living on the island and the Franciscans participated in missionary efforts to convert them to Catholicism. Sometime before 1815, a measles epidemic swept the island population. Many of the survivors relocated to mainland missions.

In 1830, the Mexican Government landed a group of exiled prisoners on the island. These enterprising convicts later made rafts and floated themselves to the mainland where they assimilated into the Santa Barbara/Ventura population.

Later, Chinese fishermen squatted along Santa Cruz shores breath-hold diving for abalone, and eventually, hard hat diving for other shellfish. Well known Santa Barbara seafarer, Captain Ira Eaton and his wife ran a resort at Pelican Bay from 1910 to 1937. Their guests included many celebrated Hollywood stars of the day, including William Boyd and John Barrymore.

The first individual to own Santa Cruz Island was Andres Castillero. He received the island as a grant from the Mexican governor of California. Castillero's deed was confirmed when California was ceded to the United States in 1864. The island was later sold to William E. Barron and transferred into the hands of several businessmen who formed the Santa Cruz Island Company.

The entrepreneurial spirit came to the islands in a big way and Santa Cruz's fertile hills and lush central valley became home to olive

Anemones make ideal targets for photographers' extension tubes.

groves, grape and vegetable fields. Ranching also prospered as sheep, cattle, horses and pigs were raised. Ranch buildings were built throughout the island; even a small chapel was erected. Santa Cruz Island also had its own winery, and bottled its own private label of Zinfandel, Chablis and Burgundy. Today, the island is still controlled by private owners, however, the National Park Service is negotiating its eventual purchase. Santa Cruz Island is currently incorporated into the boundaries of the Channel Islands National Park and marine sanctuary.

GEOGRAPHY

Modern day explorers will discover that Santa Cruz is an island of diverse terrain and topogarphy, both above and below the surface. Since the island curves eastward and resembles a roughly hewn crescent, the front side of the island faces incoming weather that blows out of the north from Point Conception. This creates the unusual characteristic where the weather side of the island actually faces the mainland. The backside, which faces open ocean, is often the calmest area as it does not receive the full force of the winds and swell coming out of the north.

The frontside of the island is covered with sloping grassy hills. After winter and spring rains, the landscape is vibrant green and the hills are dotted with bright yellow coreopsis wildflowers. The rugged backside of the island is relatively barren and foreboding with high mountain peaks to the north. Sierra Blanca on the backside of the island crests at over 1,500

feet. Devil's Peak on the Santa Barbara Channel side of the island towers over 2,400 feet in height. In extremely cold years, snow has fallen on these island mountains.

DIVING

The average diver visiting the Channel Islands will discover that Santa Cruz offers much in the way of varied terrain and marine life. There are many terrific diving areas on the island of which the following sites are just a small sampling.

63. FORNEY'S COVE (S)

DEPTH:	10-50 FEET
LEVEL:	NOVICE TO EXPERIENCED

Forney's is the last sheltered diving and anchoring area on the northwest end of Santa Cruz Island. Protected from wind by the high headlands near Frazer and West Point, the area is ringed by a series of small islets that provide relief from incoming swell. At Forneys, dive boats can anchor in stillwater while only 100 yards beyond, the wash rocks of the infamous "Potato Patch" are boiling.

The only disadvantage to tucking inside Forney's during periods of dicey weather is that visibility is reduced. Despite this fact, good diving still remains, for in cloudy waters with only 10- to 15-foot visibility, divers still enjoy hunting for large red abalone among the shallow rocks and finding halibut in the sand. Under calm conditions, water clarity can increase to 30 feet. Forney's is often a "last dive of the day spot," giving divers the opportunity to go on one last halibut foray or soak up a little sun, stow gear, and prepare for the often rough journey through the Potato Patch and around the northwest corner of the island. Once the west end of Santa Cruz Island

Large red abalone and halibut are the targets for hunters at Forney's Cove, while photographers search for the pelagic moon and purple jellyfish that are often found here.

is cleared, the run home to Santa Barbara is with the prevailing wind and swell astern.

When conditions are marginal, most photographers rinse off their cameras and pack them securely for the ride home. Yet when the waters are calm and relatively clear, as they can be from time to time, Forney's is an excellent spot to photograph a wide variety of tealia and corynactus anemones, sea stars, reef fish, and gorgonian fans. Due to Forney's extreme northwestern position, pelagic creatures such as miniature jellyfish are often found in the cove. These pelagic cnidarians such as the moon jellyfish and purple jellyfish provide excellent subjects in the shallow cove. Some are small enough to accommodate large extension tube framers.

Other highlights of Forney's are the pelicans and cormorants which roost on the outer islets and on the wash rocks that protect the kelp-lined cove. Depths inside the cove average 25 feet, but are shallower close to shore. At the entrance to the cove divers will find 50-foot depths and small rocky reefs that are good producers of abalone. A beautiful sandy beach lines the inside of this rocky cove, making Forney's one of Santa Cruz Island's most picturesque spots.

64. MORSE POINT

DEPTH:	45-75 FEET
LEVEL:	NOVICE TO INTERMEDIATE

Morse Point is approximately one mile west of Gull Island and the towering summit of Sierra Blanca, a huge, pyramid-shaped mountain looming in the center of Santa Cruz's seaward side. Several wash rocks extend seaward at Morse Point, which combined with the dense surface kelp, generally result in stillwater, even when an afternon breeze is kicking up out of the northwest.

The reef starts in 45 feet of water and drops off into sand at 75 feet. The entire area slopes seaward. The reef system is characterized by long finger-like extensions and small pinnacles, and is loaded with nudibranchs and other invertebrates. Watchful photographers will encounter bright blue, thick-horned

aeolids, prolific sea lemons and ring spotted dorids, as well as a variety of other miniature marine creatures. Numerous neon orange cup corals cover sheets of rock, while sculpin, rockfish and an excellent representation of sea stars abound. Colorful tube and sand rose anemones are scattered throughout the area where the reef meets the sand.

Many of the small pinnacles found at Morse Point sit closely together, forming channels and canyons for divers to swim through. Kelp grows atop the summits of these. The reef system is extensive and runs a good distance offshore towards Gull Island. Calico bass, rubberlip perch, sheepshead and blacksmith are common in the area. Visibility averages 30 to 40 feet, though on calm, sunny days it can improve strikingly. Due to the size of the reef system at Morse Point, it is possible to move the dive boat to another position in the same area and experience different terrain and sea creatures.

65. GULL ISLAND

DEPTH:	20-110 FEET
LEVEL:	INTERMEDIATE TO EXPERIENCED

This small outcropping can be found a little over a mile offshore from Punta Arena which is southeast of Morse Point. Here, a series of large guano-covered rocks are home to a contingent of California sea lions, pelicans, and of course, sea gulls. Visibility at Gull Island is often excellent, averaging in the 60- to 80-foot range, and the thick surrounding kelp bed makes for a very picturesque dive.

During periods of foul weather, Gull Island is often the northern most dive site available at Santa Cruz. Because of this, the site is under heavy pressure from lobster hunters and now rarely produces a legal sized "keeper." Occasionally, a boat load of anxious lobster slayers intent on punching northward to Santa Rosa Island will often cringe in disgust when rising at daybreak to discover they are anchored behind the protection of Gull Island with a cold 30-knot wind gusting sheets of frigid water over the railing of the boat. Almost as if knowing no lobsters will be taken here,

76. THE *CHICKASAW*

DEPTH:	5-20 FEET
LEVEL:	ADVANCED
TYPE:	FREIGHTER
SUNK:	1962
LENGTH:	459 FEET

The Chickasaw, a former WW II auxiliary transport, ran aground in 1962 during her final days as a cargo ship. The rusting hulk is safest viewed from a dive boat due to her deteriorating condition.

Moving farther west to Cluster Point is a site that is more of a side trip than dive area. Sitting in the surf line with rusting edges and sharp angles protruding skyward is the wreck of the freighter *Chickasaw*. This wreck is probably the most heavily photographed piece of rusting metal in the northern Channel Islands. As an auxiliary transport during World War II, she carried troops in the Atlantic Ocean and Mediterranean Sea. Following wartime service, the *Chickasaw* reverted to a cargo carrier until running aground at Cluster Point in 1962 enroute from Japan to Wilmington, California with a load of toys.

Although the majority of the *Chickasaw* is above water, the absence of portholes in the stern quarter indicates that divers have penetrated the dangerous shallows and conducted some clandestine salvage.

Over time, the ship has been hewn in half by the pounding sea, leaving only the precarious stern section and bow remaining. Due to the severe deterioration, it is unsafe to visit the ship. But when experienced from the relative safety of a charter boat, the *Chickasaw* is a great photo opportunity. Each year, the vessel continues to deteriorate. Collecting photos of the old freighter as it undergoes its demise is an interesting study of the sea's relentless reclamation of man-made structures.

77. TALCOTT SHOALS

DEPTH: 50-80 FEET

LEVEL: INTERMEDIATE TO EXPERIENCED

A well known area frequented by lobster divers, Talcott Shoals is located on the northwestern end of the island and faces San Miguel Channel. There is much more than just lobsters to be found here.

Thoroughfare ledges. Talcott forms a series of stair-step ledges that run for miles, each ledge cascading downward into deeper water. It has been joked that this is the hardest place in the world for a diver to get lost, as the local terrain resembles elevation markings on a topographical map. The ledges are referred to as thoroughfares that run off into the distance like underwater highways. All a diver needs to do is follow one ledge for half of the dive and then move to a shallower ledge and return back to the point of origin.

Like most of Santa Rosa, this area is lush with invertebrate life. Colorful thick-horned and pugnacious aeolid nudibranchs inch their way along the encrusting corals and cobalt blue sponges. Wine colored spotted rose anemones grow in profusion amidst large orange-mantled scallops. After a severe storm, dislodged scallops can be found laying on the bottom for divers to scoop up with little effort.

At deeper depths, large rockfish lay along the bottom showing off their highly photogenic colors and textures. There are China, vermilion, gopher, olive and copper rockfish to be seen here. Using coloring as protective camouflage, these fish are easy subjects for the photographer to stalk and frame. By the same token, this situation puts them at a distinct disadvantage for the underwater hunter with a pole spear. Consequently, these delectable varieties of fish have graced many a dinner table.

Sea stars are also encountered. Some varieties divers will observe are bat, leather, rainbow and fragile rainbow, and multi-armed sunflower stars. Talcott is a large area with a wide variety of terrain and provides options for divers of all interests.

78. CARRINGTON POINT (S)

DEPTH: 15-55 FEET

LEVEL: INTERMEDIATE TO EXPERIENCED

Carrington Point is at the extreme north side of Becher's Bay and faces the mainland. When wind is out of the northwest and swells are present, it is not a good anchorage or dive site. When calm conditions prevail, however, Carrington's offers excellent opportunities for photographers and game hunters.

Its extensive reef system is rarely dived. Sparse kelp grows throughout the area, and lobster and abalone are usually plentiful.

Giant black sea bass. Scallops, and colorful nudibranchs often reside in the area, as do resident black sea bass that are protected by law. Some specimens may live more than 100 years and grow to seven feet long. At maturity, they can weigh over 500 pounds. Once nearly hunted to extinction in California, black sea

A sharp eye is often rewarded with a special find such as this giant green anenome.

CHAPTER XIV   SAN MIGUEL ISLAND

Refer to map on page 25.

Seemingly the most foreboding and desolate within the Santa Barbara Channel Island Archipelago, the weather beaten island of San Miguel is a paradox at best. Frequent gales carve and sculpt the irregular headlands and shift sand dunes in fashions that constantly change. To the naked eye it's a lonely and barren place.

Throughout the island's interior, low vegetation sways over in the breeze. Eerie limestone casings stand where prehistoric tree forests once existed. All is silent except the sound of the usually blowing wind and the surging sea pounding the rocky shoreline.

HISTORY

San Miguel Island is endowed with a significant place in history. Some of the earliest human remains of West Coast man have been found here. Archaeological remains give evidence of hundreds of Indian sites that once existed. The majority of these are thought to have been Chumash. Juan Rodríguez Cabrillo was the first European explorer to land at San Miguel in 1542. Due to the fierce winds and swells prevailing out of the north, Cabrillo and his two small ships—*San Salvador* and *La Victoria*—found it necessary to spend an entire winter at Cuyler Harbor.

Throughout history, the island has been tagged with a variety of names by the early explorers who encountered it. The Chumash called the island *Tuqan*. Cabrillo originally named Santa Rosa and San Miguel, *Los Islas de San Lucas* (the Islands of Saint Luke) and later, *La Posesion*. Neither name bestowed by the European explorer remained on the permanent charts.

History records that Cabrillo himself died due to injuries sustained during a fall on San Miguel. After badly fracturing his arm near the shoulder, Cabrillo and his crew saw an opening in the weather and beat their way northward as far as Cape Mendocino before turning back. His expeditionary force returned to their safe and familiar anchorage at San Miguel where he died from his injuries on January 3, 1543.

Although there is disagreement on whether Cabrillo was buried on the island or on neighboring Santa Rosa, his crew affectionately named the island, Juan Rodríguez in his honor. Today a small monument with a cross erected on the island honors the Portuguese navigator who gave his life in the service of Spain.

San Miguel Island gets its present name from Spanish Colonel Miguel Costanso, an engineer surveying the Channel Islands in 1770.

San Miguel was never officially deeded to colonial settlers during the Spanish and Mexican period. Because no individual held title to the island, it passed into possession of the U.S. Government in 1848 at the signing of the Treaty of Guadalupe Hidalgo. After the aboriginal inhabitants disappeared or assimilated into the mainland Indian population, a long line of squatters claimed the island to be theirs by right of possession. Later, the island was leased from the U.S. Government for sheep ranching.

During World War II, the Navy used the island for aerial bombardment as part of the Pacific Missile Range. Since many valuable archeological sites were damaged during bombing practice, scientific and environmental groups protested and eventually live firing upon the island was discontinued. In 1963, the Navy and the Department of the Interior entered into a cooperative agreement that gave the National Park Service custodial responsibilities at San Miguel.

Corynactus anemones are a welcome sight for all divers. This group surrounds a barnacle.

GEOGRAPHY

San Miguel Island is theorized to have originally been connected with Point Conception and Santa Rosa Island thus forming a singular land mass. At the very least, theorists argue that during the Ice Age, San Miguel, Santa Rosa and Santa Cruz were all connected. Proponents of this theory call the peninsula, or "super island," Santa Rosae.

One item of evidence in support of these theories is the remains of dwarfed mammoths (a prehistoric elephant) found on San Miguel and Santa Rosa. It is believed that animals and early Indians migrated to Santa Rosae during a period when the water level was much lower. As Ice Age glaciers melted, the water level rose, cutting off the peninsula and resulting in the offshore islands.

The island is roughly eight miles long by four miles at its widest point. San Miguel Island is low in elevation, the tallest point reaching 831 feet. The large peaks, canyons and ridges found on other islands are not present here.

A trip to the dive sites surrounding this harsh and desolate island is amply rewarded by San Miguel's magnificent underwater pinnacle formations. Photo: Courtesy of the National Park Service.

The surrounding water surges with shallow reefs and exposed pinnacles. Combined with fog that often blankets the area, the island is a ready made trap for producing shipwrecks. Throughout recorded history, numerous vessels have come to grief on the low-lying shoals near Point Bennett.

DIVING

San Miguel receives the full force of the northern winds banking southward off Point Conception, and so for divers, a trip to San Miguel Island can be a 50-50 proposition. The wind and swell that batters this seaward outpost is often strong enough to keep even the best and largest dive boats at bay. When fair weather does prevail, this remote arena where the elements collide unveils aquatic treasures unique among all the Channel Islands.

Although San Miguel can, at times, be inhospitable to visitors, it offers what many consider to be the finest diving within the northern island group. Weather permitting, the skies can be blue and clear with flat and smooth seas. During the fall months, air temperatures are exceptionally comfortable and sometimes hot. Underwater visibility is often spectacular as oceanic currents move

down the coast, flooding the area with clear, blue water.

These rich currents carry plankton and other minerals that benefit filter feeding organisms. Consequently, a profusion of invertebrate life thrives in San Miguel's waters. Colorful arrays of anemones, orange- and green-mantled scallops, sea stars and large red abalone find these waters to their liking.

Divers should take note that at times, this current can also bring a curse. When too much plankton blooms, the water can turn rootbeer brown, obliterating visibility.

San Miguel is also home to Stellar sea lions, elephant seals, Guadalupe fur seals, pelicans and cormorants.

San Miguel Island hosts a plethora of excellent dive sites. Of all the members of the northern group, perhaps no singular island is as well endowed with magnificent offshore pinnacles as San Miguel. Each dive boat captain working the northern islands has a small collection of personal favorites.

83. WILSON'S ROCK

DEPTH:	20-100+ FEET
LEVEL:	EXPERIENCED

Located two miles off the northwest side of San Miguel, Wilson's Rock breaks the surface in a foaming boil of surge and brine. It is a site only accessible on very calm days. This small, isolated, reef system is best characterized by steep walls that plummet hundreds of feet beneath the surface. The drop-offs are covered with iridescent purple and pink hydrocorals. Rainbow, purple and green spined starfish adorn cracks and crevices while large scallops are found in the deeper reaches. Large red and white rose anemones, tube worms and sweeping barnacles add diversity and vividness to the incredible display of marine life.

There are several small rolling crests and razorbacks that branch out. These are shallow at the top, but plunge seaward in short order.

Clown, pugnacious aeolid and sea lemon nudibranchs combine with an incredible display of sea stars to cover the rock like an ornately decorated Persian rug. Hiding among the camouflaged crevices are myriads of rockfish: China, gopher, yellow, copper, vermillion, and more. Additionally, divers will find large lingcod, cabezon and painted greenlings.

On a deep dive, an explorer may encounter a strange and elusive monkey-faced eel coiled on top of a rock.

Since Wilson's Rock has been heavily dived over the years, the shallow ledges show evidence of damage. Barren clumps of reef identify where large scallops once thrived. Broken chunks of coral reveal the legacy of careless and over-weighted divers with poor buoyancy control. Visiting divers should take care to practice good diving techniques to prevent further damage and allow the reef to regenerate.

The relatively pristine sections of Wilson's Rock can be found at 100- to 120-foot depths. While bottom time is limited, the memory and intensity of the area's beauty will last long after the wet suit is packed way.

When no plankton blooms are present, visibility can exceed 100 feet. Due to its position in the open ocean, surge and current is common, so dive cautiously. If calm enough, use the dive boat anchor line as an ascent and descent reference point and navigate forward of the boat. Use the anchor line when returning as well. A safety stop is always a good idea for all dives deeper than 60 feet.

Caution. Divers should pay extra attention to depth and air supply when diving Wilson's Rock as it is easy to drop too deep.

84. RICHARDSON'S ROCK

DEPTH:	20-130 FEET
LEVEL:	EXPERIENCED

Simply stated, if you liked Wilson's Rock, Richardson's will really impress you. It is an experience often told in stories long after the initial dive. There's just one difficulty: getting there.

Richardson's Rock lies eight miles northwest of San Miguel Island in the open ocean. It is a lonely, wave-battered islet rarely dived in comparison with other sites at San Miguel.

Divers making it to San Miguel should always consider themselves fortunate. Divers making it to Richardson's Rock should be reverent. In addition to its isolation, the Rock is usually veiled by foul weather, which adds to the boat captain's dilemma. A dive here provides a glimpse of what many of today's more commonly dived sites once looked like.

This steep-sided, wave-swept land mass is a haul out for sea lions and occasionally Guadalupe fur seals. Its deep drop-offs host some of southern California's most intense diving. When conditions allow boats to venture to Richardson's, visibility is usually stupendous. Fed by clean, clear, oceanic currents, excellent water clarity contrasts the bright red, purple and vermilion anemones that inundate the rocks. The ledges at Richardson's drop sharply from a shallow shelf to sheer walls that plummet downward into the gloom. Constant surge from rambling ocean swells precludes shallow diving even on the calmest days. Consequently, divers usually begin their exploration in waters of 60 feet or deeper.

The water is generally a stark, cobalt blue. Masses of rainbow, purple and green spined starfish drape across the rocky ledges. Huge scallops, red and white rose anemones, tube worms, and feeding barnacles add diversity and vividness to the incredible display of living creatures. It is difficult to find a solitary place to set one's hand as almost every square inch is covered by some kind of living organism.

Photographer's delight. Photographers will enjoy an absolute field day. With more than enough subject material to keep busy, it is hard to decide which lens to use. If you have more than one camera, be sure to bring them both—with different lenses.

Anemones and starfish vary in size, texture and color. Brightly decorated rockfish hide inside ledges and crevices. The branching gorgonians and bluewater backgrounds will not be disappointing.

Caution. As with Wilson's Rock, fortunate divers visiting Richardson's Rock need to consider the presence of current and surge. Large swells usually prevent diving this rocky outpost. When a light surge is present, divers can easily access deeper water to avoid it, but careful attention should be paid to avoid going too deep. Current can also scream through the area, offering the unwary diver a fast, one way ticket to Japan.

85. SIMONTON COVE (S)

DEPTH:	30 FEET
LEVEL:	INTERMEDIATE TO EXPERIENCED

Simonton Cove is a large stretch of sand in the 30-foot range west of Harris Point and March Rock. Kelp and reefs are sparse in the area. Simonton's claim to fame is that it is often an excellent producer of large halibut. With acres of sand to swim through, Simonton is a desert at best—not the type of place photographers are overjoyed at visiting. In fact, Simonton is usually where the photographers sit on the deck and outgas some additional nitrogen.

Large halibut. This is a game dive—hog heaven for halibut hunters. Depth and terrain are relatively predictable. A few small reefs dot the interior of the Cove and some kelp patches grow here. The rest is sand. From May to July, divers have been known to bag halibut of 30 to 40 pounds or more in this area, sometimes bringing back several in a single dive. Free divers also have remarkable success working the shallows. Visibility varies depending on conditions but is usually in the 15- to 40-foot range.

86. CUYLER HARBOR

DEPTH:	30-50 FEET
LEVEL:	NOVICE TO INTERMEDIATE

When conditions are calm with no swells and northerly winds, excellent diving can be encountered close to San Miguel's sandy shores. Located between Bay and Harris Point, with Prince Island near its entrance, Cuyler Harbor hosts an area of diversity that makes it popular among divers. The Harbor offers rocky reefs, generous patches of kelp and fields of fine white sand.

Divers can drift through the 30- to 50-foot depths suspended in dreamlike conditions while in awe of the area's rugged natural beauty. Bat rays settle onto the desert of fine sand along the bottom. On the reef, colorful vermilion rockfish and mottled lingcod blend into the stony substrate. Pacific electric rays boldly cruise the narrow corridors between reefs.

Photographers find an assortment of anemones, sea stars and sedentary cabezon, easily captured within the zone of their viewfinders. Large red abalone saddle the rocky ledges, while California and barn-door size Pacific halibut (a huge variety of halibut) can be uncovered hiding in the sand beyond the reefs.

87. WYCKOFF LEDGE (S)

DEPTH:	10-120 FEET
LEVEL:	INTERMEDIATE TO EXPERIENCED

Almost exactly opposite of Cuyler Harbor on the southwest side of the island is a classic example of small wall diving in San Miguel. Wyckoff Ledge is often sheltered from the prevailing northwest winds and seas that often buffet the island. Mild ocean currents generally produce excellent visibility.

Divers will encounter tremendous concentrations of marine life growing along the vertical faces of steep ledges. Like most of San Miguel's best spots, a dazzling representation of scallops, sea stars, anemones and other colorful invertebrates grows along the walls.

Depths range from ten feet in the shallows to 120 feet on a sandy plain that slopes off the base of the ledge. Ocean whitefish, occasional barracuda, varieties of mackerel and other pelagics are often encountered in the blue water a short distance beyond the drop-off.

Wyckoff Ledge can also be an excellent vantage point for migrating gray whales during winter months. Occasionally, the whales will come in close to the island, giving photographers the opportunity to shoot whales on the surface with a mere 35mm lens!

88. POINT BENNETT FOUL AREA

DEPTH:	15-50 FEET
LEVEL:	EXPERIENCED

Since the Point Bennett area is part of the San Miguel Island Ecological Reserve, access is restricted to boaters at certain times of the year. From Castle Rock (northwest) around the corner to Judith Rock (southwest), boats may not enter within 300 yards of shore without a permit. Boaters may approach within 100 yards of shore from March 15 to April 30 and October 1 to December 15.

This is due to the extensive pinniped rookery at Point Bennett. Depending on the season, a large contingent of California sea lions, Stellar sea lions, harbor seals, northern fur seals, northern elephant seals and Guadalupe fur seals may be observed at a distance along the island's shores. All breed on the island except the Guadalupe fur seal. When anchored at Tyler Bight in the evening, it is easy to hear the yelping and barking from this beach bound choir.

Point Bennett is a seething wash of low-lying rocks and razor-sharp reefs that protrude from the waterline at low tide—hence the name "foul area." This is not the place to bring a large boat. Charter vessels will anchor outside Point Bennett in deeper water and allow divers to snorkel to the dive site. Although long surface swims are necessary in this case, Point Bennett can produce large lobster, scallops and occasional halibut.

The water is often extremely clear due to ocean currents running down the island, and it is blessed with a varied population of fish and invertebrates making this site one that photographers and underwater hunters alike will appreciate. When calm, Point Bennett offers exceptional diving without having to venture deeper than 30 to 40 feet.

Caution: great white sharks. Point Bennett has been affectionately nicknamed "Shark Park" and for good reason. Because of the area's prolific sea lion and elephant seal population, Point Bennett has a small contingent of unsavory residents: namely *Carcharodon carcharias*, commonly known as the great white shark. Pinnipeds rate high on

CHAPTER XV   MARINE LIFE

A diverse and fascinating array of marine life inhabits the waters surrounding California's offshore islands. It is beyond the scope of this book to provide a complete account of these fishes, invertebrates, mammals and plants. For a detailed description we recommend *California Marine Life* by Marty Snyderman. Listed below are some of the most common marine life that divers are likely to encounter.

Jack Mackerel (Trachurus symmetricus) can engulf divers in massive schools. These schools often signal the presence of yellowtail jack and barracuda, which swim along the school's perimeter looking for an easy dinner.

FISHES

Blue Sharks

Blues *(Prionace glauca)* are pelagic sharks that grow up to 12 feet in length. Their streamlined bodies make them the perfect underwater gliding machines. Though rarely seen swimming at high speed, they are one of the fastest sharks. Dark blue coloration on their backs and a white underbelly provide them with a form of camouflage when seen from above or below. These majestic creatures are not often seen near the shore of any island, requiring divers to venture into the open ocean to observe them.

Moray Eel

California moray eels *(Gymnothorax mordax)*, often surrounded by grooming cleaner shrimp, are common in the southern islands, and sparse in the colder water of the northern islands. Divers can expect to encounter morays at Santa Barbara, Santa Catalina and San Clemente Islands. Morays must constantly open and close their mouths to push water across their gills, and though this lends to their fierce image, they are generally harmless unless provoked.

Rockfish

This copper rockfish is just one of the 62 species of rockfish (family Scorpaenidae) found throughout California's coastal waters. Rockfish go through many changes of color. In some species significant changes occur in the shape and number of spines with increasing age.

Sheepshead

Sheepshead *(Pimelometopon pulchrum)* are a colorful and much sought after game fish. A hermaphrodite species, born female, all change eventually to males. Found throughout the reefs and kelp forests of the Channel Islands, they may grow up to 3 feet and weigh 36 pounds or more.

INVERTEBRATES

California Spiny Lobster

This glory hole of California spiny lobster *(Panulirus interruptus)* is every bug hunter's dream! These lobsters live inside rocky crevices during the day and come out at night to scavenge for food. Lobster in California can only be taken by hand; pole spears or lobster loops may not be used. A legal-sized lobster may weigh 3 or 4 pounds. Some "monster" lobsters have weighed in at over 15 pounds!

Corynactus Anemones

Clusters of red and white corynactus anemones *(Corynactus californica)* are often found in deeper water in areas swept by abundant current. These filter-feeding organisms come in many colorful variations including purple and lavender hues.

Metridium Anemones

These beautiful Metridium anemones *(Metridium senile)* thrive in areas with high current velocity and colder water. They are mostly found at deeper depths, and in the bays of northern California. They are just one of the many species of colorful anemones found off the California coast.

Spanish Shawl Nudibranch

The colorful plumes on top of the Spanish shawl *(Flabellinopis iodinea)* are actually exposed respiratory organs. The word "nudibranch" is derived from Latin for "naked gill." There are over 160 species of nudibranchs divided into four suborders.

Thick-Horned Aeolid

The thick-horned aeolid *(Hermissenda crassicornis)* is another variety of nudibranch common on the offshore islands where strong currents provide ample nutrients. Nudibranchs are grazers and all are hermaphroditic.

KELP

Bull Kelp

This species of kelp is commonly referred to as "bull" kelp *(Nereocystis leotkeana)* due to its large leaves that are horn-like in appearance. Bull kelp grows in deeper water and can become quite large. It is found in all the islands.

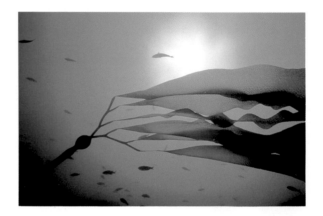

Giant Kelp

Macrocystis pyrifera, or "giant" kelp, grows as much as two feet a day from depths of 100-300 feet. They dominate the largest kelp forests, and support an incredible variety and number of marine species for which they provide food, protection and points of attachment.

California Sea Lion

Common on most of the offshore islands is the California sea lion *(Zalophus californianus)*. This one dives amidst a bed of giant kelp. Sea lions appear to enjoy playing with divers and will often look into goody bags, nibble on fins and admire their reflection in the dome ports of camera housings. As opposed to seals, sea lions have external ears, and propel themselves with their front flippers, using their hind flippers as rudders. Bulls can attain weights of 700 pounds and reach lengths of 10 feet.

Elephant Seal

Largest of the pinniped residents, these elephant seals *(Mirounga angustirostris)* are lying on the beach at Santa Barbara Island. Males can reach 16 feet and weigh 5,000 pounds. Females, which lack the male's large snout, can pack almost a ton in up to 11 feet of length. A male may keep a harem of over 30 females, and is fiercely protective of them and his territory. Elephant seals should be treated with great caution whether underwater or on shore.

Harbor Seal

Harbor seals *(Phoca vitulina)* are distinctively different from sea lions. They are somewhat shyer to approach and have smaller bodies, small front flippers and a spotted coat. They will curiously follow divers on the bottom, but from a distance. When noticed, they will usually retreat. Harbor seals can weigh 300 pounds and grow to six feet in length.

APPENDIX 1

EMERGENCY NUMBERS

Divers Alert Network (DAN)	**(919) 684-8111**
Marine Radio	**Channel 16**

Baywatch (Catalina Island)
Avalon	**(213) 510-0856**
Isthmus	**(213) 510-0341**

Ventura/Santa Barbara
Los Robles Medical Center	**(805) 497-2727**
Hyperbaric chamber	**(805) 379-5559**
Emergency only	**(805) 497-3949**

Los Angeles Area
L.A. County Medic Alert	**(213) 221-4114**

San Diego Area
San Diego Life Guard Service	**911**
Also	**(619) 221-8800**

When contacting an emergency number, be sure to state your name, exact location and the nature of the emergency. Stay on the phone until the operator confirms that all the information has been received correctly. Stay on the scene to give the responding unit additional information and assistance.

If unable to be evacuated to a hyberbaric chamber by the responding unit, it is still important to access the emergency medical system. However, since many doctors are not familiar with diving accidents you should have the medical personnel consult with the Divers Alert Network (DAN). This way you will not waste valuable time before initiating treatment and can still call on the expertise of DAN's hyperbaric doctors.

Marine Radio Channel 16

The U.S. Coast Guard monitors channel 16 of the marine radio and is prepared to render emergency assistance including air or sea evacuation to a recompression chamber.

DIVERS ALERT NETWORK (DAN)

The Divers Alert Network (DAN) operates a 24-hour emergency number **(919) 684-8111** (collect calls accepted if necessary) to provide divers and physicians with medical advice on treating diving injuries. DAN also maintains up-to-date information on the locations of recompression chambers accepting sport divers. In addition, they can organize air evacuation to the nearest recompression chamber.

Since many emergency room physicians do not know how to properly treat diving injuries, it is highly recommended that in the event of an accident, you have the physician consult a DAN doctor specializing in diving medicine.

DAN is a publicly supported, not-for-profit membership organization. Membership is $25 a year and includes a first aid manual and the newsletter *Alert Diver* which discusses diving medicine and safety. DAN members are also able to buy either a $15,000 medical insurance policy for $20 a year or a $30,000 one for $25. The policy covers hospitalization, air ambulance and recompression chamber treatment for diving injuries. Divers should check with their insurance companies since many policies do not cover specialized treatment for diving accidents.

DAN's address is: Divers Alert Network, Box 3823, Duke University Medical Center, Durham, NC 27710. Their non-emergency number is (919) 684-2948.

APPENDIX 2

Catalina Express
(213) 519-1212
(800) 540-4753
Ferry service to Avalon from Long Beach and San Pedro

Catalina Flying Boats
(213) 595-5080
Seaplane service to Avalon from Long Beach

Channel Islands Adventures
233 Durley Avenue
Camarillo CA 93010
(805) 987-1301
Air transportation and overnight excursions

Helitrans
(213) 548-1314
(800) 262-1472
Round trip helicopter service from San Pedro to Avalon

Island Packers
1867 Spinnaker Drive
Ventura CA 93001
(805) 642-1398
Hiking   transportation for Santa Barbara, Anacapa, Santa Cruz, Santa Rosa and San Miguel Islands

Smuggler's Cove Overnight Sporting Accommodations
(805) 646-2513
Private hunting on Santa Cruz Island

Catalina Dive Resorts

Hotel Macrae
Edgewater Hotel
Bayview Hotel
(213) 510-2616
(800) 262-3483

APPENDIX 3

USEFUL NUMBERS

California Department of Fish and Game
(213) 590-5132

Catalina Island Chamber of Commerce
(213) 510-2266

Channel Islands National Marine Sanctuary
735 State Street
Santa Barbara, CA 83101
(805) 966-7107

Channel Islands Visitors Center
1901 Spinnaker Drive
Ventura, CA 93001
(805) 644-8157
Information on the offshore islands, including current weather reports. National Park Service trips to some islands can be arranged here.

Nature Conservancy
213 Stearns Wharf
Santa Barbara, CA 93101
(805) 962-9111
The Nature Conservancy owns most of Catalina and Santa Cruz Islands and can arrange boat trips for hiking and camping on Santa Cruz.

Santa Cruz Island Company
PO Box 23259
Santa Barbara, CA 93121
(805) 962-6591
Landing permits west of Chinese Harbor and Sandstone Point.

Sea Center
Stern's Wharf
Santa Barbara, CA 93101
(805) 962-0885
Displays and exhibits pertaining to the Channel Islands put on in conjunction with the Channel Islands Visitors Center and the Santa Barbara Museum of Natural History.

U.S. Coast Guard (Long Beach Station)
(213) 499-5200

Weather Report (24-Hour Offshore)
(213) 477-1463

APPENDIX 4

Dive Charter Boats

Santa Barbara/Ventura

Conception, Truth, Vision
(805) 962-1127
(805) 963-3564

Liberty
(805) 483-6612

Peace
(805) 658-8286

Scuba Luv'er
(800) 227-3018
(805) 496-1014

Spectre
(805) 483-6612
(805) 642-1233

Sandy Bay
(213) 828-2418

Sea Ventures
(805) 985-1100

Chieftain
(805) 652-0321
(800) 982-6906

Los Angeles

Atlantis
(213) 831-6666

Bold Contender
(818) 366-2611

CeeRay
(213) 519-0880

Charisma Encore
(213) 832-8304
(213) 326-7460

Golden Doubloon
(714) 963-4378

Magician
(213) 548-6129

Maverick
(213) 547-3824

Scuba Queen
(213) 691-0423

Westerly
(213) 833-6047

Wild Wave
(213) 534-0034

Mr. C
(213) 831-9449

Sundiver
(213) 434-1198

King Neptune
(213) 510-2616
(800) 262-3483

San Diego

America II
619-584-0742

Bottom Scratcher, Sand Dollar
(619) 224-4997

Horizon
(619) 277-7823

Shark Dives

Catalina Island Shark Adventures
(800) 677-4275

Scuba Luv'er Blue Shark Photo Expeditions
(800) 227-3018
(805) 496-1014

America II Shark Dives
(619) 224-4997

APPENDIX 5

CALIFORNIA DIVE CENTERS

Adventure Diving Center, Inc.
1451 W Arrow Hwy.
San Dimas, CA 91773
(714) 599-1997

Adventure Sports Unltd.
303 Potrero Ct. #15
Santa Cruz, CA 95060
(408) 458-3648

Adventures in Diving
1644 W 240th St.
Harbor City, CA 90710
(213) 320-2782

Adventures In Diving
31678 Pacific Coast Hwy.
South Laguna Beach, CA 92677
(714) 499-4517

Adventures Unlimited
5267 E 2nd St.
Long Beach, CA 90803
(310) 433-2204

Alexander's Trailhead
123 N Main
Porterville, CA 93257
(209) 781-8117

Allied Pacific
833 Castlewood Pl.
Pleasanton, CA 94566
(415) 523-2033

American Aquatic Adventures
1104 Scenic Dr.
Modesto, CA 95350
(209) 578-0515

American Diving
1901 Pacific Coast Hwy.
Lomita, CA 90717
(213) 326-6663

Anchor Shack
5775 Pacheco Blvd.
Pacheco, CA 94553
(510) 825-4960

Anderson's Skin & Scuba
541 Oceana Blvd.
Pacifica, CA 94044
(415) 355-3050

Antelope Valley Scuba
1430 W Ave. I
Antelope Valley, CA 93536
(805) 949-2555

Any Water Sports, Inc.
1130 Saratoga Ave.
San Jose, CA 95129
(408) 244-4433

Aqua Adventures Unltd.
2120 W Magnolia
Burbank, CA 91506
(818) 848-2163

Aqua Divers
300 N Polara Ave. Carriage Sq.
Yuba City, CA 95991
(916) 671-3483

Aqua Sports
1. 2436 E Terrace
   Fresno, CA 93703
   (209) 224-0744
2. 4687 Chateau Pl.
   San Diego, CA 92117
   (619) 569-7132

Aqua Tech Dive Center
1800 Logan Ave.
San Diego, CA 92113
(619) 237-1800

Aquatech Scuba Center
1144 S Main St.
Manteca, CA 95336
(209) 825-6520

Aqua Ventures
2172 Pickwick Dr.
Camarillo, CA 93010
(805) 674-8344

Aquarius Dive Shop
1. 2240 Del Monte Ave. & 32
   Monterey, CA 93940
   (408) 375-1933
2. 32 Cannery Row, Unit 4
   Monterey, CA 93940
   (408) 375-6605

Aquatic Center
4535 W Coast Hwy.
Newport Beach, CA 92663
(714) 650-5440

Aquatic Sports
4195 Old San Jose Rd.
Soquel, CA 95073
(408) 462-5409

Aquatics
695 W Channel Islands Blvd.
Port Hueneme, CA 93041
(805) 984-3483

Aquatics of Santa Barbara
5370 Hollister #3
Santa Barbara, CA 93111
(805) 964-8689

Argo Diving Services
P.O. Box 1201
314 Metropole Ave.
Avalon, CA 90704
(213) 510-2208

Auburn Ski Hut
585 High St.
Auburn, CA 95603
(916) 885-2232

Autrey's Underwater Sports
1328 Sunset Dr.
Antioch, CA 94509
(510) 865-6979

Avalon Aquatics
615 Crescent Ave.
Avalon, CA 90704
(310) 510-1225

Bamboo Reef Enterprises
1. 584 Fourth St.
   San Francisco, CA 94107
   (415) 362-6694
2. 614 Lighthouse Ave.
   Monterey, CA 93940
   (408) 372-1685

Big City Scuba
1720 N El Camino Real
San Clemente, CA 92672
(714) 498-3483

Bill's Sporting Goods
75 Cayucos Dr. P.O. Box 745
Cayucos, CA 93430
(805) 995-1703

Black Barts Aquatics
1. 34145 Pacific Coast Hwy.
   Dana Point, CA 92629
   (714) 496-5891
2. 24882 Muirlands Blvd.
   El Toro, CA 92630
   (714) 855-2323

Blue Cheer Water Sports
1110 Wilshire Blvd.
Santa Monica, CA 90401
(213) 828-1217

Blue Water Scuba
722 Renz Ln.
Gilroy, CA 95020
(408) 848-6864

Bluewater Diving
711 Estes
Corcoran, CA 93212
(209) 992-3632

Bob's Dive Shop
4374 N Blackstone
Fresno, CA 93726
(209) 225-3483

Bob's Diving Locker
500 Botello Rd.
Goleta, CA 93117
(805) 967-4456

Buhrow Into Diving
1536 Sweetwater Rd. #B
National City, CA 92050
(619) 477-5946

Cal School of Diving
1750 6th St.
Berkeley, CA 94710
(510) 524-3248

California Watersports
5822 Hollister
Goleta, CA 93117
(805) 964-0180

Captain Frog's Scuba
1609 S H St.
Bakersfield, CA 93304
(805) 833-3781

Captain Frog's Dive Shop
163 Academy St.
Bishop, CA 93514
(619) 873-4646

Catalina Divers Supply
Box 126 Pleasure Pier
Avalon, CA 90704
(213) 510-0330

Catalina Diving Resorts
124 Whittley Ave.
Avalon, CA 90704
(213) 510-2616

Channel Islands Scuba
1495 Palma #C
Ventura, CA 93003
(805) 644-3483

Chico Dive Center
735 Nord Ave.
Chico, CA 95926
(916) 343-2341

Chuck's Scuba School
222 W Aliso
Pomona, CA 91768
(714) 622-7232

Cimi Dive Store
P.O. Box 796
Avalon, CA 90770
(213) 510-1622

Clearwater Ocean Sports
1275 Hwy. 1
Bodega Bay, CA 94923
(707) 875-3054

Colorado River Valley Divers Sch.
2001 De Soto
Needles, CA 92363
(619) 326-3232

Coral Reef Dive Center
14161 Beach Blvd.
Westminster, CA 92683
(714) 894-3483

Del Mar Oceansports
1227 Camino Del Mar
Del Mar, CA 92014
(619) 792-1903

Depth Perceptions Diving Serv.
2360 Main St. #B
Morro Bay, CA 93442
(805) 772-3128

Desert Scuba
44441 N Sierra Hwy.
Lancaster, CA 93534
(805) 948-8883

Dive N Surf
504 N Broadway
Redondo Bch, CA 90277
(213) 372-8423

Dive Quest Inc.
2875 Glascock St.
Oakland, CA 94601
(510) 533-3483

Dive West Sports
115 W Main
Santa Maria, CA 93454
(805) 925-5878

Divers Corner
12045 Paramount Blvd.
Downey, CA 90242
(310) 869-7702

Divers Dock
696 Auzerais Ave.
San Jose, CA 95126
(408) 298-9915

Divers Exchange
649 Pacific Ave.
Alameda, CA 94501
(510) 523-5146

Divers West
2333 E Foothill Blvd.
Pasadena, CA 91107
(818) 796-4287

Divers World
1500 W 6th St. #C
Corona, CA 91720
(714) 371-3483

Divers' Supply
2501 Colorado Blvd.
Los Angeles, CA 90041
(213) 344-0036

Diver's Den
22 Anacapa St.
Santa Barbara, CA 93101
(805) 963-8917

Diver's Mart
2036 W Whittier
La Habra, CA 90631
(213) 694-1311

Diving Belle
P.O. Box 332
San Mateo, CA 94401
(415) 358-0225

Diving Center of Santa Rosa
2696 Santa Rosa Ave.
Santa Rosa, CA 95401
(707) 527-8527

Diving Equipment Co. of America
333 E Haley St.
Santa Barbara, CA 93101
(805) 564-1923

Diving Locker
1. 405 N Hwy. 101
   Solana Beach, CA 92109
   (619) 755-6822
2. 8650 Miramar #C
   San Diego, CA 92126
   (619) 271-5231
3. 1020 Grand Ave.
   San Diego, CA 92109
   (619) 272-1120

Dolphin Swim School
1520 El Camino Ave.
Sacramento, CA 95815
(916) 929-8188

Double D Systems
415 School St., Hwy. 1
Pt. Arena, CA 94568
(707) 882-2746

Empire Scuba
627 W State St.
Redlands, CA 92373
(714) 798-3483

Explorer Dive & Travel
1135 Garnet Ave.
San Diego, CA 92109
(619) 483-3120

Fantasea Connection
1925 W Walnut Ave.
Visalia, CA 93277
(209) 739-1337

Far West Marine Center
1. 1733 Los Angeles Ave.
   Simi Valley, CA 93065
   (805) 522-2628
2. 2941 Willow Ln.
   Thousand Oaks, CA 91361
   (805) 495-3600

Fish & Dive Shop
3590 Peralta Blvd.
Fremont, CA 94536
(510) 794-3474

Fremont Dive Center
41463 Albrae St.
Fremont, CA 94538
(510) 657-1004

Get Wet Inc.
2525 Morena Blvd.
San Diego, CA 92101
(619) 275-1822

Gold Coast Scuba
2464 E Main St.
Ventura, CA 93003
(805) 652-0321

Guccione's Scuba Habitat
2843 Diamond Bar Blvd. #A
Diamond Bar, CA 91765
(714) 594-7927

Harbor Dive Center
200 Harbor Dr.
Sausalito, CA 94965
(415) 331-0904

High Desert Scuba Ctr.
17153 Bear Valley Rd.
Hesperia, CA 92345
(619) 947-6938

High Sierra Divers, Inc.
1237 E Main St.
Grass Valley, CA 95945
(916) 477-7642

Howell's
1426 Eureka Way
Redding, CA 96001
(916) 241-1571

Innerspace Divers
1305 N Chester Ave.
Bakersfield, CA 93308
(805) 399-1425

Island Marine & Sporting Goods
124 Catalina Ave.
Avalon, CA 90704
(310) 510-0238

Keene Aqua Shop
1517 28 St.
Sacramento, CA 95816
(916) 451-3640

Kingfish, Inc.
957 Oliver St.
San Pedro, CA 90731
(213) 548-4138

K.L.G. Sports Center
2933 W Pico Blvd.
Los Angeles, CA 90006
(213) 735-0111

Lady Go Diva
1137 Vista Del Lago
San Luis Obispo, CA 93405
(805) 544-9140

Laguna Sea Sports
1. 2482 Newport Blvd.
   Costa Mesa, CA 92627
   (714) 645-5820
2. 6343 Magnolia Ave.
   Riverside, CA 92506
   (714) 683-6244
3. 925 N Coast Hwy.
   Laguna Beach, CA 92561
   (714) 494-6965
4. 925 N Pacific Coast Hwy.
   Laguna Beach, CA 92651
   (714) 494-6965
5. 5245 W Rosecrans
   Hawthorne, CA 90250
   (310) 643-7966

Lancaster's Sports
11205 Clara Ct.
Riverside, CA 92505
(714) 353-9819

Lane's Marine Service
11120 Atlantic Ave.
Lynwood, CA 90262
(213) 631-3506

Liburdi Scuba Center
2272 Michelson Dr. #114
Irvine, CA 92715
(714) 955-1446

Malibu Divers, Inc.
21231 Pacific Coast Hwy.
Malibu, CA 90265
(310) 456-2396

Marin Skin Diving
3765 Redwood Hwy.
San Rafael, CA 94903
(415) 479-4332

INDEX

A **bold** faced page number denotes a picture caption.
An <u>underlined</u> page number indicates detailed treatment.